DIAMONDS
in a
CARDBOARD
BOX

DIAMONDS
in a
CARDBOARD BOX

A COMMENTARY ON THE SECOND
EPISTLE TO THE CORINTHIANS

DOUGLAS WILSON

CANON PRESS

MOSCOW, IDAHO

Published by Canon Press
P. O. Box 8729, Moscow, Idaho 83843
800–488–2034 | www.canonpress.com

Douglas Wilson, *Diamonds in a Cardboard Box: A Commentary on the Second Epistle to the Corinthians*
Copyright ©2024 by Douglas Wilson

Cover design by Josiah Nance
Interior design by Valerie Anne Bost

Printed in the United States of America

Library of Congress Cataloging-in-Publication Data is on file with the publisher.

24 25 26 27 28 29 30 31 32 33   10 9 8 7 6 5 4 3 2 1

CONTENTS

This book is dedicated to
Jared and Heather Longshore, co-laborers.

INTRODUCTION

Whenever people are starved for something, they are uniquely susceptible to counterfeits. A man in the desert, dying of thirst, imagines an oasis in a mirage. If a man is hungry enough, he might eat food that is rancid. The lack or the want suppresses the levels of discernment.

We live in a generation that is starved for authenticity, and this is why there is so much inauthentic authenticity on display—everywhere we look. Centuries ago, under the influence of that rascal Rousseau, we bought into the idea that an authentic spirit is lonely and artistic, a true bohemian barely scraping by in a garret somewhere. And that is why, today, you can buy your jeans pre-ripped. There is no need to let your hair get greasy naturally by itself over time—you can buy the grease in a tube at Safeway and carefully craft whatever kind of careless bed head you want the world to see.

The human heart is a scoundrel, and whatever is honored in the surrounding culture is sure to be copycatted. Sam Goldwyn is purported to have once said, "The secret of success is sincerity. Once you can fake that, you've got it made." Sub in the word "authenticity," and you have a good description of our generation.

And this is why we could all use a good dose of 2 Corinthians. In this hot and intense epistle written to a church afflicted with spurious apostles, the apostle Paul is defending the authenticity of his ministry. In fact, the letter is an extended description of what true, authentic ministry necessarily looks like. This is something we really need in our day, because the Pauline approach is *authentically* authentic. This is the real thing. The cardboard box may be tattered, but the diamonds inside it are real enough.

There are various places in this book where my debt to Kent Hughes will be plain and obvious. His very fine commentary entitled *Power in Weakness* was a wonderful resource for me as I was preaching through this book. And that brings me to the origins of this commentary, which happen to be a series of messages to the saints at Christ Church in Moscow, Idaho, preached in the latter half of 2022 and the first part of 2023.

It is offered in the hope that you will find it edifying and that it will drive you back to the only one who can manifest His power in the midst of weakness.

DOUGLAS WILSON
Christ Church
July 2024

2 CORINTHIANS 1:1–2

The task before us is to work our way through this letter of Paul's to the Corinthians, the letter we commonly call 2 Corinthians. We call it this because we only have two letters that Paul wrote to this church, although there was almost certainly another one. The missing letter would be located in between the two letters we have.

> Paul, an apostle of Jesus Christ by the will of God, and Timothy our brother, unto the church of God which is at Corinth, with all the saints which are in all Achaia: Grace be to you and peace from God our Father, and from the Lord Jesus Christ. (2 Cor. 1:1–2)

What is the historical background? Achaia, mentioned here in this passage, is what we would call southern Greece.

Northern Greece was known then as Macedonia. Corinth was built on the Isthmus of Corinth, where the Peloponnese was connected to the mainland. Cenchrea (Rom. 16:1; Acts 18:18) was the harbor that serviced Corinth on the eastern side of that isthmus, and another harbor (Lechaeumon) serviced it from the west.

Corinth was a new city with an old name. The Corinth of classical Greece had been destroyed by the Romans in 146 B.C. and left desolate for about a century. The Romans rebuilt it in 44 B.C. and wound up making it their capital of Greece. The city was quite influential and also sexually corrupt and decadent.

When Paul first came to Corinth (around A.D. 49–50), the city was around eighty years old and had a population of about 80,000 people. The city was a *nouveau-riche* boom town, populated by merchants and other hustlers. The Corinthians were wealthy, and their wealth was manifested in trade, in sports, and in entertainment. The theater in Corinth held 18,000 people. Aphrodite was the goddess of the city, and at one time there were five temples in the area dedicated to her. According to Strabo, the earlier Greek temple to Aphrodite was staffed with a thousand sacred prostitutes, and something similar may also have been the case with the new temple in the Roman era.[1]

To plant a church in Corinth was to plant a church in a key strategic location. This was an important city, and that meant that a church there was going to be an important church.

1. R. Kent Hughes, *2 Corinthians: Power in Weakness*, Preaching the Word (Wheaton, IL: Crossway, 2006), 13–14.

This letter is a robust defense of Paul's ministry, which had been challenged at Corinth by various spurious apostles. This is why Paul begins by saying that this letter is from Paul, an apostle of Jesus Christ *"by the will of God"* (v. 1a). The letter was also from Timothy, Paul's co-laborer; it was addressed to the church of God in Corinth, not to mention all the saints throughout all of Achaia (v. 1b). Verse 2 is Paul's standard salutation: grace and peace from the Father and the Son. Following an observation of Jonathan Edwards, I believe the Spirit is not mentioned by name simply because He *is* the grace and peace, proceeding from the Father and the Son.

There was some ecclesiastical drama going on at Corinth. When Paul first came to Corinth, he ministered there for about a year and a half. Working together with Timothy and Silas, not to mention Aquila and Priscilla, the initial planting of this church was quite successful (Acts 18:1–17). After Paul left, he went to Ephesus, then to Jerusalem, then back to Ephesus. After a period of about three years, he wrote the letter that we call 1 Corinthians. There is no confusion, because 1 Corinthians was his first letter to them. Paul then sent Timothy to Corinth for a visit (1 Cor. 16:1–11).

Timothy discovered that Paul's enemies had been at work in Corinth, orchestrating a revolt against the apostle. Paul then determined to visit Corinth briefly in order to address everything. That visit was a disaster, what Paul called his "painful visit" (2 Cor. 2:1, ESV). All kinds of stories were circulating about Paul, and many of the Corinthian Christians had rejected him as a result and had gone after a "different gospel" (2 Cor. 11:4, NKJV). In addition, certain discernment blogs had identified many questionable Pauline activities (2 Cor. 2:17). Paul returned to Ephesus, wiped out, and sent Titus to Corinth with what he called his "severe" letter (2 Cor. 2:4–5, NKJV). This missing letter is the original 2 Corinthians, while our 2 Corinthians is actually 3 Corinthians. Still with me?

That missing letter called for the Corinthians to repent, and glory to God, most of them actually did. The bulk of the church came back over to Paul's side, although there was still significant cleanup that had to take place. That cleanup is the purpose of this epistle, as Paul makes preparations to come to them for his *third* visit (2 Cor. 12:14; 13:1).

In this letter, we find Paul's most extensive defense of his apostolic ministry. Paul *hated* talking about himself, but he loved the gospel so much that if a defense of gospel ministry required it, he was willing even to do that. So what is authentic ministry? How is it defined? How is it measured?

Paul tells the Corinthians in this letter that he had been flogged by the Jews five times (2 Cor. 11:24). The Mishnah tells us that the whip had three leather strands, and thirteen strokes would be applied to the chest, thirteen to one shoulder, and thirteen to the other. This happened to Paul *five times*. That is 585 welts for the kingdom.

Why is Paul emphasizing this kind of thing? Had he given up on trying to impress the Corinthians? Wasn't their problem with him the fact that Paul was so *weak* in his bodily presence with them (2 Cor. 10:10)? Yes, it was. But as Paul undertakes to teach them the true meaning of authentic ministry, part of that lesson includes learning how God loves to showcase His power in the midst of weakness. This is God's MO.

And he said unto me, My grace is sufficient for thee: for my strength is made perfect in weakness. Most gladly therefore will I rather glory in my infirmities, that the power of Christ may rest upon me. (2 Cor. 12:9)

But we have this treasure in earthen vessels, that the excellency of the power may be of God, and not of us. We are troubled on every side, yet not distressed; we are perplexed, but not in despair; Persecuted, but not forsaken; cast down, but not destroyed; Always bearing about in the body the dying of the Lord Jesus, that the life also of Jesus might be made manifest in our body. For we which live are always delivered unto death for Jesus' sake, that the life also of Jesus might be made manifest in our mortal flesh. So then death worketh in us, but life in you. (2 Cor. 4:7–12)

So take heart, Christian. In Christ, faithful weakness is our superpower.

2 CORINTHIANS 1:3–2:4

THE GOD OF ALL COMFORT

As the people of God, we are partakers of Christ's sufferings together with Him. Because of this, we are partakers of one another's sufferings. And because of *that*, we can be partakers in one another's comforts. But in order to receive the comfort that we ought to receive, the apostle's doctrine here requires some unpacking.

> Blessed be God, even the Father of our Lord Jesus Christ, the Father of mercies, and the God of all comfort; Who comforteth us in all our tribulation, that we may be able to comfort them which are in any trouble, by the comfort wherewith we ourselves are comforted of God. For as the sufferings of Christ abound in us, so

our consolation also aboundeth by Christ. And whether we be afflicted, it is for your consolation and salvation, which is effectual in the enduring of the same sufferings which we also suffer: or whether we be comforted, it is for your consolation and salvation. And our hope of you is stedfast, knowing, that as ye are partakers of the sufferings, so shall ye be also of the consolation. (2 Cor. 1:3–7)

This passage is saturated in comfort. Paul begins by blessing God, who is the Father of our Lord Jesus Christ (v. 3a). By way of apposition, this God is called the *Father of mercies* and the *God of all comfort* (v. 3b). As the God of all comfort, the Father comforts Paul and his company so that they might be able to pass on that comfort to those who are in any other kind of trouble (v. 4a). The comfort that is passed on is explicitly identified as the comfort that was received; it is the *same comfort* (v. 4b). Paul says that as the sufferings of Christ abound, so also his consolations abound (v. 5)— and then he presents a very interesting line of thought. If the apostolic band is afflicted, it is for the Corinthians' "consolation and salvation." If the apostolic band is comforted, that, too, is for the Corinthians' "consolation and salvation" (v. 6). If Paul's entourage goes left, it is for consolation and salvation. If they go right, same thing. If they remain where they are, same thing. For Paul and the Corinthians, the afflictions and the comforts are identical. Paul's hope concerning the Corinthians was therefore steadfast. Since they were partakers of the suffering, they would also be partakers of the consolation (v. 7).

In the first century, the first of the nineteen synagogue blessings began this way: "Blessed art thou, O Lord our God and God of our fathers, God of Abraham, God of Isaac, and God of Jacob." Later in that benediction, God is also called the "Father of mercies." Paul is taking those words and recasting them in order to rejoice in the Father of Jesus Christ as the God of all comfort. This recast synagogue blessing also appears elsewhere (Eph. 1:3; 1 Pet. 1:3). Remember that Paul is dealing with some Judaizing adversaries here, and so he is showing that according to his gospel, Christ is seen as the fulfillment of the Old Testament promises, and not as a mere continuation of the Old Testament system itself.

This short passage accounts for about one third of all the New Testament references to comfort. The word is used here in both noun and verb forms, and it is a peculiar kind of gospel comfort. We are servants of the suffering servant, after all, and a servant is not greater than his master (John 13:16; 15:20). If the world hates us, we should know that it hated Christ first (John 15:18). We are partakers with Him in the whole story.

Simeon and Anna both were waiting for the consolation of Israel (Luke 2:25). The Messiah Christ was the promised comfort of Israel (Isa. 40–66). This sets the stage for the comfort that Paul is talking about here. It is an explicitly *Christian* comfort. This is not a pampering comfort, but rather a Christ-comfort.

Again, the theme of this epistle is authentic ministry. The charge against Paul was that he must not be a genuine apostle. How could he be? If he had been a genuine apostle, he wouldn't be getting into so much trouble, now would he? And certainly, by any reasonable measurement, the apostle Paul appeared to be genuinely snakebit. He was one of the most afflicted men who ever lived. He lived on the lip of perpetual death: "For we who live are always delivered to death for Jesus' sake, that the life of Jesus also may be manifested in our mortal flesh" (2 Cor. 4:11, NKJV).

His was a ministry that was constantly on hairpin turns at high speeds on two wheels. Authentic ministry careening down Rattlesnake Grade. What had Paul endured? He goes into it in depth later in this epistle (2 Cor. 11:23–30). Flogged five times. Beaten with rods three times. Stoned. Shipwrecked. Hungry and thirsty, cold and naked. Jail time in various places. Should we put all this in the glossy prospectus that we send out to prospective donors? If you were on a pastoral search committee, what would you do with an application like this one? If you were looking for a spokesman for your church, is this the guy you would send out to the cameras?

We have to deal with that Old Devil Respectability. If we are biblical Christians, we should always want to maintain in our own ministries the same sorts of tensions that were evident in biblical ministries. On the one hand, we are told that an elder must have a good reputation with outsiders (1 Tim. 3:7). Sure thing. But then Jesus tells us that there is a kind of honor and respect that is a stumbling block: "How can ye believe, which receive honour one of another, and seek not the honour that cometh from God only?" (John 5:44). The apostle Paul tells the Galatians that he wishes that the false advocates of circumcision would go whole hog and cut the whole thing off (Gal. 5:12). But *in the very next verse,* he urges them "by love [to] serve one another" (Gal. 5:13–15). He tells the Philippians that he wants them to have their love abound more and *more* in knowledge and in all judgment (Phil. 1:9). The greatest of these is love! This is shortly before he calls the false teachers he was dealing with evil workers and dogs (Phil. 3:2).

So remember that authentic ministry will always have an element of the disreputable about it. Authentic ministry does not necessarily play well with others. Authentic ministry runs with scissors.

We are servants of a *crucified* Messiah. This did not happen because Jesus got along well with the established authorities. And if we accompany Him in the pathway of His sufferings, as we are called to do, we are invited to partake of all the comforts that the God of *all* comfort might offer.

WITH UPTURNED FACES

There will never come a time in your Christian life where the Spirit will invite you to coast. You are not going to grow to an age where it will be unnecessary to trust God. There will always be *something* that you need to trust God for. We never grow out of our need to believe in the God who raises the dead. There will never be as much padding as you would like.

> For we would not, brethren, have you ignorant of our trouble which came to us in Asia, that we were pressed out of measure, above strength, insomuch that we

despaired even of life: But we had the sentence of death in ourselves, that we should not trust in ourselves, but in God which raiseth the dead: Who delivered us from so great a death, and doth deliver: in whom we trust that he will yet deliver us; Ye also helping together by prayer for us, that for the gift bestowed upon us by the means of many persons thanks may be given by many on our behalf. (2 Cor. 1:8–11)

Authentic ministry is in constant need of resurrection power. Paul here alludes to some kind of monumental trouble that he and his band had encountered in Asia. Some interpreters think that this is referring to the riot in Ephesus (Acts 19:23–20:1), but Paul's description of his internal emotions here does not seem to line up with that episode. He describes himself here as despairing "even of life" (v. 8), and during that riot in Acts he was actually trying to get into the amphitheater in order to speak to the crowd. So it is best to apply this description to some unidentified disaster of Paul's life.

Now the reason Paul was given this sentence of death "within himself" was so that he might learn a lesson, that lesson being a "resurrection lesson" (v. 9): don't trust in yourself, but rather in God who raises the dead. This is the God who delivered, who does deliver, and who will deliver again (v. 10). This is the lesson. Note that it is not necessary to die "all the way" in order to learn of God's resurrection power. He can teach this lesson by taking us right to the brink and pulling us back. Abraham sacrificed his son, even though God stopped him at the last minute.

What God does in the past is to be taken by us as a pattern. What God has done we may trust Him to continue to do. An essential part of God's plan for establishing His church, fulfilling the Great Commission, and extending His kingdom throughout the world is the suffering of church planters, missionaries, and pastors. As they imitate Christ, it turns out that they imitate Him in His sufferings. This is why He has things go wrong. When things "go wrong" in this way, you should know you are on the right track.

This requires great wisdom, because there is a kind of "going wrong" that should be a signal to knock off whatever it is you are doing. The sluggard is supposed to consider his lazy ways and amend them (Prov. 6:6–10). The prudent man watches his step (Prov. 14:15), as well he should.

So how can we tell that we are suffering because we are on the right track, and not because we are being foolish? How can we know that the reason for all the antiaircraft fire is that we are over the target? The answer is that you are to know the options because you know the Scriptures—learn how to use them as a help to reading the story you are in, and then walk by faith. Afflictions can be God's stop sign, and they can also be His blinking yellow. Walk in wisdom. Walk in faith.

We must proceed as we have been invited—we begin by faith, and we continue our walk by faith. But this faith is not blind faith. We are looking to the Word. A skeptic is going to say that "just because something happened in the past doesn't mean it will happen again." And what are we to make of the variations in the promises of God? He says that He will not allow the wicked to succeed in killing the

righteous (Ps. 37:32–33), and yet what about Dietrich Bon-
hoeffer? In that same psalm, God promises provision during
famine (Ps. 37:19). Has no believer ever died of starvation?

We should always appeal to Hebrews 11:32–39, and then
look at the stark transition in the middle of verse 35. Some
of God's people received their dead back to life. Others were
tortured. Some conquered, others were conquered, and all
did so in faith. The promises of God are not theorems from
Euclid, where triangles will never not have three sides. The
promises are rocks in God's quarry, and as you build your
house, you need to decide with intelligence and faith which
rocks you will use. Read your Bibles constantly and, having read your Bibles, read the story you are in. Do this hon-
estly—take your thumb off the scales. If your thumb is on
the scales, you are not building a scriptural house. Rather,
you are just daydreaming and weaving Bible verses into it.

That said, He delivered us in the past. He will deliver us
in the immediate future. And He will certainly deliver us in
the ultimate future.

This is why we come to God with upturned faces. Paul's
final thought here gives us a biblical basis for getting a lot of
people to pray for something. The Corinthians had clearly
helped Paul through their prayers—the gift of deliverance was bestowed through the prayers of many, meaning
that there would also be gratitude offered up to God from
the many (v. 11). The apostle Paul was not at all shy about
requesting prayer. This is not because he doubted the sov-
ereignty of God—it was because he *did* believe in the sov-
ereignty of God. Answered prayer is one of the central tools
that God uses to teach us that everything proceeds from Him.

Paul requested prayer for continued boldness (Eph. 6:19). He requested prayer for deliverance (Phil. 1:19). He prayed that a door for effective ministry would open (Col. 4:3). He requested prayer for the Word of the Lord to speed on and be honored (2 Thess. 3:1). Paul requested many prayers from many saints, and he did this a lot.

We get more details about how this should work in verse 11. The Corinthian saints were helping Paul by praying for him. When the gift of answered prayer was bestowed on Paul and his company, it was by means of the prayers of many faces (*prosopon*). Think of many faces, uplifted to Heaven on Paul's behalf—and when God answers their pleading, those same faces may look toward God in deep gratitude.

Prayers do not ascend to Heaven as so many data points, conveying mere information, with angels counting returns as though it were election night. God does not answer prayers so much as He answers faces. Prayer and its answers are a conversation. Prayer is a relationship. Moreover, it is a covenanted relationship, bound together in the name of the Lord Jesus Christ. And the more the merrier. Whenever we worship God in the name of Jesus Christ, God loves seeing our faces. So lift up your heads. We are in Christ, and in Christ we are summoned to ask God to regard our faces.

THE YES OF GOD

Christ must be worshiped by us as the ultimate *yes*, but we must come to understand rightly how this works. God does not come down and make promises to us directly. Rather, He makes promises throughout all of Scripture, promises that are given generally to His *people*, and also to individuals (like Abraham) who are covenant representatives of His people. These promises are bestowed on the people of God, and as we read these promises, or hear of them, we join together with those people, identifying with them by faith, and God joins us to them by joining us to Christ—through the imputation of Christ's righteousness, justifying us. What is our relationship to the promises then?

> For our rejoicing is this, the testimony of our conscience, that in simplicity and godly sincerity, not with fleshly wisdom, but by the grace of God, we have had our conversation in the world, and more abundantly to you-ward. For we write none other things unto you, than what ye read or acknowledge; and I trust ye shall acknowledge even to the end; As also ye have acknowledged us in part, that we are your rejoicing, even as ye also are ours in the day of the Lord Jesus.
>
> And in this confidence I was minded to come unto you before, that ye might have a second benefit; And to pass by you into Macedonia, and to come again out of Macedonia unto you, and of you to be brought on my way toward Judaea. When I therefore was thus minded, did I use lightness? or the things that I purpose, do I purpose according to the flesh, that with me there should be yea yea, and nay nay? But as God is true, our word toward you was not yea and nay. For the Son of God, Jesus Christ, who was preached among you by us, even by me and Silvanus and Timotheus, was not yea and nay, but in him was yea. For all the promises of God

in him are yea, and in him Amen, unto the glory of God by us. Now he which stablisheth us with you in Christ, and hath anointed us, is God; Who hath also sealed us, and given the earnest of the Spirit in our hearts.

Moreover I call God for a record upon my soul, that to spare you I came not as yet unto Corinth. Not for that we have dominion over your faith, but are helpers of your joy: for by faith ye stand.

But I determined this with myself, that I would not come again to you in heaviness. For if I make you sorry, who is he then that maketh me glad, but the same which is made sorry by me? And I wrote this same unto you, lest, when I came, I should have sorrow from them of whom I ought to rejoice; having confidence in you all, that my joy is the joy of you all. For out of much affliction and anguish of heart I wrote unto you with many tears; not that ye should be grieved, but that ye might know the love which I have more abundantly unto you. (2 Cor. 1:12–2:4)

Remember the context. Paul's severe letter has quelled the rebellion against him at Corinth, but there is still some cleanup to do. Here, he begins to address specific charges.

Paul starts the process by rejoicing in the fact that his conscience is clear (v. 12), both toward the outside world and toward the Corinthians. Authentic ministry is at odds with "fleshly wisdom" and is characterized by *simplicity* and *sincerity*. The Corinthians should already know this (v. 13). They have acknowledged that in the day of Christ, both they and Paul will be engaged in mutual rejoicing. But they have only come partway along, which is why this cleanup is necessary (v. 14).

Now we get to the complaint Paul is answering. Paul's previous intention had been to visit the Corinthians on the way to Macedonia, and then to visit again on his way back to Judea (vv. 15–16). But he changed his mind and wrote the severe letter instead. Was he vacillating or temporizing in this? Not at all (vv. 17–18). Paul reminds the Corinthians that the gospel of Christ that *he* preached to them, along with Timothy and Silvanus, was not a "yes and no" gospel (v. 19). All the promises of God are "yes" and "amen," to the glory of God, *"by us"* (v. 20). He reminds them that *God* is the one who joined them all together through His anointing (v. 21). The Spirit is God's gift: a sealing work and an earnest payment (v. 22). In this context, Paul gives the reason he had not come to Corinth: he did not want to be their disciplinarian in person (v. 23). His more appropriate role was to be a "helper of their joy" rather than wielding dominion over their faith—because it is by faith that we stand (v. 24).

So Paul had decided against another personal visit if it was going to be a heavy one (2 Cor. 2:1). If he became a grief to the Corinthians, then who would be there to make him glad (v. 2)? And so he wrote to them instead, in order to preserve their relationship (v. 3), and his choice had clearly been wise. He tells them here that his severe letter had been written in turmoil and anguish, and not in *order* to grieve them. Rather, it was a testament to how much he loved them (v. 4).

Once a revolt against authority is underway, *whatever* that authority does will be seized upon and rolled into the argument. This is the spirit of carping criticism. If Paul had gone left, he would have been assailed for not going right. If he had gone right, he would have been pilloried for not going left. Remember that apostolic ministry is personal, and opposition to it is also personal. Paul then reminds the Corinthians how unambiguous his declaration of the gospel had been. His steadfastness was personal as well.

It's true that a temporizing traveler is going to be a temporizing man, and a temporizing man is going to sound like one in the pulpit. Paul's argument here is not an argument of deflection. It is not as though he was charged with embezzling funds (as he probably actually was—1 Cor. 16:1–4; 2 Cor. 11:7–10, 12:16–17), and he then tried to respond with, "Isn't the gospel *grand*?" No. It is possible for the gospel to be glorious and for a particular preacher to be a skunk.

What Paul is arguing here is that the charges against *him* are not plausible, that the kind of sneakiness he was being charged with was not consistent with what the Corinthians knew about him. He is not defending himself with an abstract gospel in the sky, but rather with a potent gospel as it had been preached on the ground. God had brought glory down through *him* (v. 20), and the Corinthians had been there when it happened.

In all of this, Paul is not defending his own person or guarding his own fragile ego. If somebody wants to gather up some glory for himself, but leaves the truth alone, Paul doesn't mind (Phil. 1:15–18). But he will fiercely defend himself if the target of the slander is the ministry and message itself (Gal. 1:17–24).

Was Paul a hard and severe person? When roused, Paul could be hard as nails. When the gospel was at stake, he could be immovable (Gal. 1:8). He had been hard on the Corinthians in his severe letter (2 Cor. 2:2–4). But this had been much against his personal desire or inclination. There is a school of pastoral care that could be characterized as the "Hang 'em high" school of thought, with "Why not now?" as the immediate afterthought. Paul did not belong to this school.

The apostle Paul here exults in the true nature of gospel light. Christ is the *yes* of God. Christ is the *yes* and *amen* of God. Sin is the *no* of the devil. The devil is the accuser, the devil is the killjoy, the devil is the one telling you how awful you are—and with no relief in sight. The Spirit convicts in order that He may comfort. The devil accuses in order that he may bite and tear.

So Christ is therefore the ultimate *yes*—the only *yes* that sinners can have.

2 CORINTHIANS 2:5-17

THE AROMA OF LIFE

One of the basic lessons of Scripture is the lesson of gospel inversion. Humility exalts. Servanthood rules. Death lives. The underdog triumphs. The back of the line is the front of the line. And it does not matter how many times we are taught this principle; we always have to come back and learn it afresh every morning.

> But if any have caused grief, he hath not grieved me, but in part: that I may not overcharge you all. Sufficient to such a man is this punishment, which was inflicted of many. So that contrariwise ye ought rather to forgive him, and comfort him, lest perhaps such a one should be swallowed up with overmuch sorrow.

Wherefore I beseech you that ye would confirm your love toward him. For to this end also did I write, that I might know the proof of you, whether ye be obedient in all things. To whom ye forgive any thing, I forgive also: for if I forgave any thing, to whom I forgave it, for your sakes forgave I it in the person of Christ; Lest Satan should get an advantage of us: for we are not ignorant of his devices.

Furthermore, when I came to Troas to preach Christ's gospel, and a door was opened unto me of the Lord, I had no rest in my spirit, because I found not Titus my brother: but taking my leave of them, I went from thence into Macedonia. Now thanks be unto God, which always causeth us to triumph in Christ, and maketh manifest the savour of his knowledge by us in every place. For we are unto God a sweet savour of Christ, in them that are saved, and in them that perish: To the one we are the savour of death unto death; and to the other the savour of life unto life. And who is sufficient for these things? For we are not as many, which corrupt the word of God: but as of sincerity, but as of God, in the sight of God speak we in Christ. (2 Cor. 2:5–17)

To stay oriented, the man that Paul is urging the Corinthians to forgive in these verses is the man who led the rebellion against Paul in the congregation there at Corinth. This should *not* be considered as referring to the incestuous man who took up with his stepmother in 1 Corinthians. Paul begins by saying that if this man has caused grief, it was mostly to the church, and not to him personally (v. 5).

There had apparently been a vote in which the majority returned to Paul, and afterward they inflicted punishment on this ringleader and troublemaker. Paul says that this punishment is sufficient (v. 6). He then urges the church to forgive and comfort this man, lest he be overwhelmed (v. 7). The rebels against Moses had been swallowed up by the earth (Num. 16:31–34), but the rebel against Paul was not to suffer that fate, not if Paul could help it. Reaffirm your love for him, Paul says (v. 8). Paul had written to the Corinthians in order to test them. Now that they had passed the test, it was time for forgiveness (vv. 9–10)—and the requirement to forgive this man was yet one more test. Paul agrees to forgive anything that they might forgive, in the presence of Christ, lest Satan take advantage of them and stir up even more acrimony (v. 11). You all *must forgive* (Col. 3:12–13). A refusal to forgive this man would mean that they were being beguiled by Satan, whose wiles in this area are many. He throws fiery darts, and he hands out candies—he accuses sinners, or he flatters them, depending on the situation. We resist him with forgiveness and with discipline, also depending on the situation.

Next Paul gives the Corinthians a bit of personal history. After Titus had been sent off to Corinth with the hot letter, Paul had gone to Troas (north of Ephesus, toward Macedonia). The door for ministry there was wide open (v. 12)—but because Titus was not there with any news, Paul went on to Macedonia (v. 13). And after an agonizing wait there (2 Cor. 7:5–7), he eventually got the good news back from Corinth. And so now he breaks into a *very different* kind of exultation—and it really is quite a strange one.

God leads Paul in triumph in Christ and diffuses knowledge of Himself like a fragrance (v. 14). Paul's band of co-workers is the fragrance of Christ, to both the saved and the perishing (v. 15). One group reacts to it like it is the smell of death upon death, and the other as though it is life upon life (v. 16). Who is sufficient for these things (v. 16)? The answer is no one. And this is the measurement of authentic ministry—our theme throughout this epistle, remember. Paul does not hawk or peddle the gospel of God, like others do, but rather speaks sincerely in the sight of God in Christ (v. 17).

Paul takes a custom of the Romans, the triumphal procession, and works it into a striking metaphor. When a victorious general was given a triumph, he led a parade in a chariot drawn by horses, and sometimes by elephants. He was clothed in purple and held an eagle-crowned scepter. His face was colored or tinted red, in order to evoke the name and power of Jupiter. There were musicians and pagan priests burning fragrant incense that wafted out over the crowd, and mountains of treasure, and prows of ships, and a horde of prisoners in native costume bringing up the rear—who were all then executed at the conclusion of the parade. This is what God did to the principalities and powers (Col. 2:15).

But in *his* use of the metaphor, Paul occupies an unexpected spot. He is at the end of the procession. He is one of the prisoners, led by God in triumphal procession. He is not the conquering general, but rather God is the general, and Paul is the captive.

Recall that one of the themes of this epistle is that authentic ministry is characterized *by suffering*.

Always bearing about in the body the dying of the Lord
Jesus, that the life also of Jesus might be made manifest
in our body. (2 Cor. 4:10)

As unknown, and yet well known; as dying, and, behold, we live; as chastened, and not killed. (2 Cor. 6:9)

Paul knew what it was to die daily in ministry (1 Cor.
15:31). And this is why Paul could speak with such authority.

The gospel is never available for $19.95. When Paul says
here that he does not "peddle" the Word of God (v. 17,
NKJV), the original word has the connotation of huckster-
ism—a merchant with his thumb on the scale, or a wine
merchant who cuts his product with a little water. The sinner is not shopping for an attractive salvation, one that is
arranged nicely in the shop window and reasonably priced.
No, the gospel is free, and to many of the passersby, it
stinks. Nevertheless, this is still the message that will conquer the world. Who is sufficient for these things? And yet,
somehow, this message preached by impotent and suffering
messengers is profoundly potent. For the carnally minded,
the real mystery is why this itinerant minister, pelted with
rocks everywhere he went, was eventually going to have
cathedrals in those same regions named after him.

This is the authority of forgiveness. So the apostolic band
takes a pounding and is dragged along behind the procession, in the sight of a gawking crowd. Paul takes the lead in
dealing with this dishonor, and it is one of the great myster-
ies of the gospel as to why this is so inexorably *attractive*. It
exudes an aroma—to the elect the aroma of life, and to the

godless the aroma of death. In search of the answer to that question, we come back to the beginning of this passage, where Paul is requiring the Corinthians to *forgive* the man who had led the revolt against him. Forgiveness—everyone in this messed up world needs it. Forgiveness—apart from grace, everyone in this messed up world hates it.

This is the radicalism of the cross. This is the salvation of Christ, and the way of Christ.

2 CORINTHIANS 3:1–18

THE EXTERNAL LETTER

We are now coming to a passage that teaches us where the spiritual action really is. Do you want to be right with God? It is not going to happen because you got all your papers in order and then got them stamped. "Right with God" *is* a judicial category, but not a bureaucratic one.

> Do we begin again to commend ourselves? or need we, as some others, epistles of commendation to you, or letters of commendation from you? Ye are our epistle written in our hearts, known and read of all men: Forasmuch as ye are manifestly declared to be the

epistle of Christ ministered by us, written not with ink,
but with the Spirit of the living God; not in tables of
stone, but in fleshy tables of the heart. And such trust
have we through Christ to God-ward: Not that we are
sufficient of ourselves to think any thing as of ourselves;
but our sufficiency is of God; Who also hath made us
able ministers of the new testament; not of the letter,
but of the spirit: for the letter killeth, but the spirit
giveth life. (2 Cor. 3:1–6)

Paul asks the Corinthians, "Are you really going to make
me talk about myself? Are you going to make me address
things that you already know?" (v. 1). Paul says that *they*
are his walking, living, breathing letter of recommendation
(v. 2), written on the hearts of the apostolic company. The
tablets are human hearts, and the writing utensil is not a
pen or a chisel, but rather the Spirit of God (v. 3)—and the
Corinthians themselves are the letters that are inscribed.

Paul then states his confidence (v. 4), which is toward God
in Christ. The same Paul who just a few sentences before
cried out *who is sufficient?* now says that, while he is not sufficient *in himself*, he is nevertheless sufficient through God
(v. 5). God is the one who has made him a minister of the
new covenant—not of the letter, but of the Spirit. The letter
kills, but the Spirit gives life (v. 6).

Every finite servant of God has a breaking point. Think of
Gandalf and the Balrog. That is what it means to be finite.
And because God *tests* His servants, He needs to take them
right up to that limit. Why? Well, remember chapter 1 verse
9: "But we had the sentence of death in ourselves, *that we*

should not trust in ourselves, but in God which raiseth the dead." God wants to squeeze *all* the self-sufficiency out of His servants. "You, my son, are still entirely too perky." Some men are too talented for God to use, at least in their current condition, but absolutely no one is too weak for God to use.

When you are exhausted and virtually tapped out, this is the moment for God to move. Did Jeremiah feel sufficient (Jer. 1:6)? Did Moses feel sufficient (Exod. 4:10–17)? Did Ezekiel feel sufficient (Ezek. 1:1–3:11)? Did Gideon feel sufficient (Judg. 6:15)? Did Isaiah feel sufficient (Isa. 6:1–7)? Did *Paul* feel sufficient (2 Cor. 16)? Who is sufficient for these things?

By the same token, and for the same reason, we see that Paul had supreme confidence in his sufficiency in Christ. "Our sufficiency is *of God*" (v. 5). In other words, when you come to the end of yourself, you have not come to the end of Christ. Coming to the end of Christ's reserves is not even a possibility.

Why does Paul say that the letter kills? The problem with "letters that kill" is not the fact that they are letters. The letters written on our hearts are letters. This epistle of 2 Corinthians was written with letters.

The problem with "letters that kill" is also not the one who wrote them. We're told in Exodus that the Ten Commandments were written by the finger of God:

And he gave unto Moses, when he had made an end of communing with him upon mount Sinai, two tables of testimony, tables of stone, written *with the finger of God.* (Exod. 31:18; cf. Deut. 9:10)

And we see elsewhere in Scripture that the finger of God is equated with the Holy Spirit:

> But if I with *the finger of God* cast out devils, no doubt the kingdom of God is come upon you. (Luke 11:20)

> But if I cast out devils *by the Spirit of God*, then the kingdom of God is come unto you. (Matt. 12:28)

God is involved in all of it. The Spirit of God gives us His Word. The Spirit of God is the one who forms the letters, wherever they are inscribed—whether outside the sinner or inside the saint.

The problem with "letters that kill" is *where* the letters are written. When they are written on stone, external to the sinner, *out there*, they do nothing but condemn—and the truer they are, the more condemnation they bring. When the law is "out there," the law is my adversary. When the gospel is "out there," the gospel is also my adversary.

When the truth of God is simply *out there*, in a leather-bound Bible, on your shelf, then your heart is still as black as that Bible's cover.

The condition that determines the destiny of every person is the regenerate or unregenerate state of every human heart. And it is one or the other. The unregenerate heart is wrecked by everything divine. The law condemns him (Gal. 3:11), and the gospel is the aroma of death to him (2 Cor. 2:16). The regenerate heart is nourished by everything divine. The law of the Lord is perfect, converting the soul (Ps. 19:7). The gospel is the aroma of life to those who are being saved (2 Cor. 2:16).

The unregenerate man always wants his religion *out there*, where he can manipulate it, defend it, control it, argue about it, and orchestrate riots on its behalf. He does this for Diana of the Ephesians (Acts 19:28, 34), and he does it for the temple of Jehovah in Jerusalem (Acts 21:29). And it is worth noting that the name of the real god in these two instances was Mammon, a substantial god that a man can manage and handle. The riot in Jerusalem was set off because they jumped to conclusions about Trophimus the *Ephesian*, wanting to make him feel right at home. "We have religious riots in Ephesus too."

So the life-and-death issue is not the presence of truth. Rather it is the presence of truth in the inner man. As the saying goes, too many miss Heaven by eighteen inches—the distance between the head and the heart. "Behold, *thou desirest truth in the inward parts*: and in the hidden part thou shalt make me to know wisdom" (Ps. 51:6). Keeping the true religion out there is the way to turn it into a false religion.

So the *external* letter kills, but the Spirit brings life. And one of the things the Spirit brings life to *is* the letter. He does this by inscribing His letters on the human heart. The heart is the only place where the letters written by the Spirit—on stone, or papyrus, or wax, or printed paper—can come to life.

Remember that Paul begins this section by saying that the *Corinthians* were written on his heart. When God writes His law on our hearts, something remarkable happens. Not only is *thou shalt love thy brother* written on your heart, but your brother *himself* is also written on your heart. *Love your neighbor* is condemnation when it is engraved in stone, or on a plaque, or in a devotional, or stuck on the fridge. But when God brings it home to you, He does not just engrave a proposition *about* your neighbor on your heart, but He engraves your *neighbor* on your heart. And this can only happen because Christ was engraved there first.

When the law is internalized, it brings the sinner to life. And when the law is internalized, this brings the letters to life. What happened to the handwriting of ordinances that was against us? God gathered it up and nailed it to the cross (Col. 2:14). But what happens to anything that is nailed to the cross of the Lord Jesus Christ? That is right—it rises from the dead. The only thing that doesn't rise again is the sin itself. But the law? The condemnation? The black despair of never being good enough? The accusations? All of that is "nailed to the cross, and I bear it no more, praise the Lord, praise the Lord, oh, my soul."

That law that used to condemn you is raised again with you and is now your liberty, your refreshment, your pleasant instructor. His name is Jesus Christ.

LETHAL GLORY

We have now come to what might be called the crescendo of the great new covenant symphony. The overture was glorious, but it nevertheless fades in our memory as we listen to the portion of the performance that God has brought us to now.

> But if the ministration of death, written and engraven in stones, was glorious, so that the children of Israel could not stedfastly behold the face of Moses for the glory

of his countenance; which glory was to be done away: How shall not the ministration of the spirit be rather glorious? For if the ministration of condemnation be glory, much more doth the ministration of righteousness exceed in glory. For even that which was made glorious had no glory in this respect, by reason of the glory that excelleth. For if that which is done away was glorious, much more that which remaineth is glorious.

Seeing then that we have such hope, we use great plainness of speech: And not as Moses, which put a vail over his face, that the children of Israel could not stedfastly look to the end of that which is abolished: But their minds were blinded: for until this day remaineth the same vail untaken away in the reading of the old testament; which vail is done away in Christ. But even unto this day, when Moses is read, the vail is upon their heart. Nevertheless when it shall turn to the Lord, the vail shall be taken away. Now the Lord is that Spirit: and where the Spirit of the Lord is, there is liberty. But we all, with open face beholding as in a glass the glory of the Lord, are changed into the same image from glory to glory, even as by the Spirit of the Lord. (2 Cor. 3:7–18)

Before summarizing the text, we need to begin with a correction of a common misconception about this passage. That misconception is that Moses put a veil on his face in order that the Israelites would not realize how transient his radiance was. The misconception occurs because of a mistranslation of a verb that occurs three times here (vv.

7, 11, 13). In this understanding, the radiance of Moses' countenance drained like a battery, and he would go into the tabernacle to meet with God, in order to recharge his face. This is not correct; the verb used here (*katargeo*) does not actually have the meaning of "to fade away." Rather, the children of Israel could not look at the glory of the ministry of death, a ministry that was going to be rendered inoperative or made obsolete.

The law was a ministry of death. Graven in stones, external to the heart, all it could do was kill you. Nevertheless, this killing law was still glorious, and the Israelites couldn't even look at it (v. 7). This glory, the glory of the law, was to be done away with. How much more glorious, Paul says, will the ministry of the Spirit have to be then (v. 8)? If the ministry of condemnation was glorious, how much surpassing glory would the ministry of imputed righteousness need to have (v. 9)? Like a bright moon that fades when the sun rises, the former glory will pale in comparison (v. 10). If the *temporary* ministry of condemnation was glorious, why would the *permanent* ministry of imputed righteousness not be much more glorious (v. 11)? All of this is the basis of Paul's plain speaking (v. 12). Paul could do what Moses couldn't, which was to administer the glory that both ministries had (v. 13). Israel couldn't even look at their glory. The reason was that their minds were blinded, down to Paul's day. For them the veil remained in the reading of the law, but the veil is removed in Christ (v. 14). He repeats the point: down to his day, when Moses is read, the veil is *on their hearts* (v. 15). When they turn to Christ, the veil is lifted (v. 16). The Lord is the Spirit who brings the liberty of being able to handle glory (v. 17). But we, like Moses in the tabernacle, worship the Lord with unveiled faces and are ourselves transformed by the work of the Spirit (v. 18).

The common reading that I rejected a moment ago makes Moses a manipulator and deceiver: he didn't want the people to realize that his glory was not permanent, and so he hid the fading of that glory away.

But here is the original narrative:

> And it came to pass, when Moses came down from mount Sinai with the two tables of testimony in Moses' hand, when he came down from the mount, that Moses wist not that the skin of his face shone while he talked with him. And when Aaron and all the children of Israel saw Moses, behold, the skin of his face shone; and they were afraid to come nigh him. And Moses called unto them; and Aaron and all the rulers of the congregation returned unto him: and Moses talked with them. And afterward all the children of Israel came nigh: and he gave them in commandment all that the LORD had spoken with him in mount Sinai. And till Moses had done speaking with them, he put a vail on his face. But when Moses went in before the LORD to speak with him, he took the vail off, until he came out. And he came out, and spake unto the children of Israel that which he was commanded. And the children of Israel saw the face of Moses, that the skin of Moses' face shone: and Moses put the vail upon his face again, until he went in to speak with him. (Exod. 34:29–35)

The passage in Exodus doesn't have any hint of Moses trying to hide the fact that his radiance would fade. He wore the veil because his radiance was frightening to the children of Israel, and it was hard for them to come near. This is the ministry of *death*, remember, according to Paul. Moses hid his face, not to encourage their hopes, but to allay their fears. The law is not sin, but the law *is* death to sinners. Recall that two chapters earlier, in the aftermath of the golden calf fiasco, three thousand Israelites had been killed (Exod. 32:26–28)—and God had told them in just the previous chapter that He would not go with them, lest He wind up having to consume them in the way (Exod. 33:3, 5). Moses was veiling them from a glory that was lethal, a glory that kills.

So what is Paul's illustration about then? Moses was not being deceptive about the glory that would fade, but some of his ostensible heirs most certainly *were* being deceptive about it. Whenever the law was read, the unbelieving Jews could not see the condition of their Ichabod-hearts. The veil covered the face, and in Paul's illustration here, the heart is the face (v. 15). They could not see the true condition of their heart. When the law was being read, a veil of unbelief was over their heart, preventing them from seeing what the law was saying about their heart.

But we, with open face (that is to say, open heart), are looking straight at the glory of the Lord in the gospel. We are in the same position as Moses during his visits to the tabernacle. This is why we are being transformed from glory to glory. God is giving us the "light of the knowledge of the glory of God in the face of Jesus Christ" (2 Cor. 4:6).

2 CORINTHIANS 4:1–18

PREACHING BRIGHT BLUE

A faithful proclamation of the gospel of Christ brings in disputes and challenges. There are unbelievers, many of them very clever, who say that what we are claiming is ridiculous. We are charged to go into a country filled with people who have been blind from birth, and we are told that our message is to be "bright blue." How is it possible for this to work?

> Therefore seeing we have this ministry, as we have received mercy, we faint not; But have renounced the hidden things of dishonesty, not walking in craftiness, nor handling the word of God deceitfully; but by manifestation of the truth commending ourselves to

every man's conscience in the sight of God. But if our
gospel be hid, it is hid to them that are lost: In whom
the god of this world hath blinded the minds of them
which believe not, lest the light of the glorious gospel
of Christ, who is the image of God, should shine unto
them. For we preach not ourselves, but Christ Jesus
the Lord; and ourselves your servants for Jesus' sake.
For God, who commanded the light to shine out of
darkness, hath shined in our hearts, to give the light of
the knowledge of the glory of God in the face of Jesus
Christ. (2 Cor. 4:1–6)

In these verses, we must remember that Paul is still
picking up the pieces after a revolt against his authority
in Corinth. Some really serious allegations had been made
against him, which Paul here flatly denies. He begins by
declaring that he and his companions have no intention
of becoming discouraged in their ministry, because they
have already received mercy (v. 1). He had not been dishonest, he had not been sneaky, and he had not handled
the Scriptures deceitfully (v. 2). He was able to commend
himself to every man's conscience. And if someone doesn't
see *gospel* in what Paul is saying, it is only hidden from the
lost (v. 3) and is out of their sight because of blindness (v.
4a). That blindness is the result of the god of this world,
the devil, blinding the minds of unbelievers, lest gospel
light shine on them. That gospel is glorious because it is
the gospel of Christ, who is the image of God (v. 4b). The
preached Word must be from outside ourselves. Paul does
not preach himself, he says, but rather Christ the Lord (v.

5). As a corollary, he says they are servants to the Corinthians for the sake of Christ (v. 5). This salvation is the creative work of God, who regenerates sinners in the same way He created light on the first day (v. 6). He says, "let it happen," and it happens. So what does He command for our hearts? The light of the knowledge of the glory of God in the face of Jesus Christ (v. 6).

Our message is light, and the challenge is that the people we preach to are blind. Christ is the light of the world (John 1:9; 8:12). He came into the world in order to shine on every man. We come to the slumbering unbelievers and summon them to wake up (Eph. 5:14).

But there is a necessary process here. Christ appeared to Paul on the Damascus road and commissioned him . . .

> . . . to open their eyes, and to turn them from darkness to light, and from the power of Satan unto God, that they may receive forgiveness of sins, and inheritance among them which are sanctified by faith that is in me. (Acts 26:18)

There are three steps for the evangelist here. The first is to open eyes, which is done through preaching the law. Once they are aware of the need, and that they are in the dark, the second step is to turn them toward the light, which is the light of the gospel. The third step is to be a midwife to the actual transfer, leading the person to Christ.

Much gospel preaching is shedding light on the blind. Much moral teaching opens people's eyes to their need, but then gives no light. When the first two things happen, and in this order, the third thing happens—people are converted. As we preach law and light, a marvelous thing happens. As we minister in obedience by His grace, God gives out eyes.

Remember: we become like what we worship. The plain statement of that principle is here, in verse 6. As we look to Christ, as He is, we are in the process of becoming like Christ, as He is.

Paul has said before that he does not preach himself. *He* is not the message. Our lives are where the message lands, not where the message originates. And the message that is set before us is "the light of the knowledge of the glory of God in the face of Jesus Christ" (v. 6). This is what we see when we look at Christ straight on, as He is preached in a gospel that is preached straight on.

But we are also told in verse 4 that *Christ* is the image of God (v. 4). This means that as we worship God through the face of Jesus Christ, the image of God is being restored in us. We were initially created in the image of God, of course (Gen. 1:27), and the *remains* of that image are still about us (Gen. 9:6). But when we fell, that image was marred, thoroughly wrecked. Our first parents fell, or more properly, they crashed, and we are the debris field.

The restoration of the image of God in man is why Jesus came (Eph. 4:23–24). His mission is to make us complete human beings again (Col. 1:15–20).

How does this happen? It happens as we look to Him. Look to Christ on the cross, to Christ in the bread and wine, to Christ in your brothers and sisters, and to Christ in the gospel. Always look to Christ.

A CARDBOARD BOX FULL OF DIAMONDS

The persistent and obvious weakness of God's servants is not a bug, but rather a feature. God does it this way because He wants us to glory in Him and not in ourselves. If we were to win the battles all on our own, we would be tempted to trust in ourselves. But God wants us to trust in Him as the one who raises the dead. If we lapse into trusting in ourselves, we are trusting in a power incapable of raising the dead—and in a world like ours, that's no good.

> But we have this treasure in earthen vessels, that the excellency of the power may be of God, and not of us. We are troubled on every side, yet not distressed; we are perplexed, but not in despair; Persecuted, but not forsaken; cast down, but not destroyed; Always bearing about in the body the dying of the Lord Jesus, that the life also of Jesus might be made manifest in our body. For we which live are alway delivered unto death for Jesus' sake, that the life also of Jesus might be made manifest in our mortal flesh. So then death worketh in us, but life in you. (2 Cor. 4:7–12)

Earthen vessels—clay pots—were the cardboard boxes of the ancient world. They were used to store anything and everything. In Paul's metaphor, the excellencies of God are like pearls and diamonds, and our lives are a cardboard box that God has decided to put them in (v. 7). Paul has shifted from the metaphor of light to the metaphor of treasure. He then moves on to describe how beat up the cardboard box was (v. 8).

All of his comparisons are meant to describe how the box remained functional, despite having gone through a lot. The box was still able to hold what it held. Troubled, but not distressed (v. 8a). Perplexed, but not despairing (v. 8b). Persecuted, but not abandoned (v. 9a). Down, but not out (v. 9b). Always carrying the death of Christ *on* the box so that the life of Christ might be seen *within* the box (v. 10). Coming at the same idea from another angle, Paul says that death has tattered the box to such an extent that the resurrection gems inside it can be seen (v. 11). The more beat-up the box, the easier it is to pull down the sides and see the diamonds. Paul then adds a surprising twist—the death works in the apostles, but the life he is talking about resides in the *Corinthians* (v. 12). They were, as it were, part of Paul's internal glory (v. 12).

We should learn to think of our weaknesses as God's copper. Just as copper wire conducts electricity, so also man's frailty conducts the power of God. Anyone who has ever touched an exposed hot wire is learning something about the power of electricity, and only secondarily learning something about the nature of copper.

Paul was squeezed but not squashed. As one translator puts it, he was "bewildered, but not befuddled."[1] He was persecuted by men, but never abandoned by God. He was knocked over, but not knocked out. His enemies came close to getting him at Lystra, when they stoned him in the city, dragged what they thought was his corpse outside the city limits, and left him there for the birds. But when they were

---

1. R. Kent Hughes, *2 Corinthians: Power in Weakness*, Preaching the Word (Wheaton, IL: Crossway, 2006), 92.

gone, and the disciples were standing around his body, Paul opened his eyes and said, "We done here?" He then got up and went *back into the town* (Acts 14:19–20). What a *mensch*.

The afflictions of those who are closely following Christ are not haphazard. They are not random. They are not meaningless. They are not pointless. On the contrary, they are *the* point. How else can the copper conduct the electricity unless it is strung into wire?

Still, when afflictions and trials are barreling down on us, it is easy to give way to *anxiety*. We are constantly juggling cares, responsibilities, obligations, possible disasters, and tenuous relationships, all while anticipating the entire, threatening process of death. But in the epistle to the Philippians, Paul says that we are to be anxious "for nothing; but in every thing by prayer and supplication with thanksgiving" we should present our prayers to God (Phil. 4:6). He then says that the peace of God will protect us (Phil. 4:7).

There are two crucial things here. First, we shouldn't be worrying on our knees. Worry and anxiety are not sanctified just because we give way to them in a posture of prayer. The key is *thanksgiving*. Sing a psalm, and hand it over to God. Hand it over to God, and then sing a psalm.

Second, the peace of God is not some frail thing that needs protection. Rather, it's the great shield of God that *does* the protecting. What needs protection are our "hearts and minds" (Phil. 4:7). To say the same thing another way, you do not protect your helmet with your head.

Fruit-bearing is a function of substitution, and we are called to imitate the Lord in this. It is not just suffering, but rather suffering *for others*.

Now some people assume that as Christ is the only one who can die as a fully efficacious substitute, then that must mean that we do not participate in any kind of substitutionary exchange at all. We think that Christ is the only one who could suffer "for others." But this is false. Remember what Paul says here—death was in him, and life in the Corinthians (v. 12). Husbands are to love their wives as Christ loved the church and gave Himself up for her, and this results in their ability to wash her with the water of the Word (Eph. 5:25–26).

Paul also says that in his sufferings, he fills up the remainder of Christ's sufferings (Col 1:24), which means there is some kind of a connection. And Jesus tells us plainly that unless a grain of "wheat fall into the ground and die, it abideth alone: but if it die, it bringeth forth much fruit. He that loveth his life shall lose it; and he that hateth his life in this world shall keep it unto life eternal" (John. 12:24–25).

So we do not *duplicate* what Jesus did, but we are commanded to *imitate* it, and God is pleased in His grace to make that imitation efficacious. Imitating the ultimate fruitfulness is fruitful.

And so Christ sets the pattern of "my life for yours." But He sets the pattern so that we might follow His example. And as we follow His example, He is pleased to enable us to "bear much fruit." We are *Christians*. This is the Way.

LIGHT AFFLICTION

We read in the book of Job that man is born to trouble as the sparks fly upward (Job 5:7). This being the case, we need to learn how to handle these troubles rightly, for we *will* have them. They are not optional. There are no exceptions. What do you call a man who has a lot of money, and a sunny disposition, and good digestion, and a photogenic family, and a shelf stacked with trophies and assorted other honors? Well, one name for him is "worm food." This is the only way to reckon the value of everything "under the sun."

But there is another calculus, introduced to the world three days after the crucifixion of Jesus.

> We having the same spirit of faith, according as it is written, I believed, and therefore have I spoken; we also believe, and therefore speak; Knowing that he which raised up the Lord Jesus shall raise up us also by Jesus, and shall present us with you. For all things are for your sakes, that the abundant grace might through the thanksgiving of many redound to the glory of God. For which cause we faint not; but though our outward man perish, yet the inward man is renewed day by day. For our light affliction, which is but for a moment, worketh for us a far more exceeding and eternal weight of glory; While we look not at the things which are seen, but at the things which are not seen: for the things which are seen are temporal; but the things which are not seen are eternal. (2 Cor. 4:13–18)

Paul has the same spirit of faith as Christ, and so he speaks the same way the psalmist did. He believes, and therefore he speaks (v. 13). This is cited from Psalm 116:10. True heart-belief is connected to the tongue. Paul then turns to reason from the certainty of the Lord's resurrection to the certainty of his own resurrection. The one who raised up Jesus will raise up Paul and his companions and will present them all together with the Corinthians (v. 14). Everything is for their sake, Paul says, so that abundant grace might redound to the glory of God through the thanksgiving of many (v. 15).

Widespread gratitude in a community of saints is potent. Grace produces gratitude, and gratitude produces abundant grace, which glorifies God (v. 15). This truth is what keeps Paul going. He does not faint (v. 16a). The outward man might be getting beat up, but the inner man is getting younger every day (v. 16b).

Remember that Paul was one of the most afflicted men who ever lived. He certainly had gone through countless troubles. But how does he describe affliction here? He calls it "light" and "momentary" (ESV). It will pass in a minute. And on top of that, Paul says this light affliction "worketh for us" a much weightier thing: the eternal weight of glory (v. 17). So gratitude works abundant grace, and affliction works its weight in glory. The key, Paul says, is to keep your eyes off what you can see, in order to fix your eyes on what you cannot yet see (v. 18a). Why? Because the things you can see you will only be able to see for a minute—they are temporal (v. 18). Yesterday is now ghostly. What was so real a moment ago turns out to have been momentary. And the eternal things you cannot see now are things you will be able to see forever and ever (v. 18b).

But Paul is not kidding himself. When Paul calls his afflictions "light," this is not because he is delusional. He knows very well the weight of his afflictions. Talking about how pressed and pushed down he was, he earlier referred to the weight of his troubles in Asia (2 Cor. 1:8). He is not a block of wood, and no stoic. He is not arguing that his pains are nonexistent or trifling. Rather, he is telling us, by faith, that his pains fade *in comparison* to something else. He refuses to weigh his troubles in isolation. He evaluates his life, and the troubles in it, by the video and not by the snapshot.

This is a typical Pauline turn of mind. In Romans, he says that our present sufferings are *not worth comparing* to the glory that will be revealed in us (Rom. 8:18). You put the glory of the resurrection on one side of the scales, say, ten bricks of gold, and then drop twenty or so lead molecules of affliction on the other side. That is the kind of thing Paul is doing. This is not a stiff upper lip approach. Paul is calculating and comparing, not muscling through. But in order to do this you have to be able to see the coming glory, and this is only possible with the eye of faith.

But Paul is not saying that bad things happen down here, and then good things happen later, up there in a completely different realm, and so it all evens out somehow. Rather, our coming glory is the *bloom* of our current afflictions. These afflictions are the instruments that God uses to bring the other about: "Our light affliction, which is but for a moment, *worketh for us* a far more exceeding and eternal weight of glory." As the cue ball puts the eight ball in the corner pocket, so your troubles are laboring industriously for your gain. They are your friends. They are your very best friends. You ought to be nicer to them. They are remodeling contractors, come to renovate your soul. They showed up right on time, 8 a.m., and they all have crowbars in their gloved fists, and that kitchen is going to be fabulous when they are done. Your afflictions are the dust all through the house. So this is why you need to count it all joy when you meet various trials (James 1:2)—you can see what is coming (James 1:3–4). This is why we are to *glory* in tribulations (Rom. 5:3). This is why, when you are tempted to look at your demolished kitchen in despair, you are instructed to go pull out the designer's rendering and then rejoice in the chaos (Rom. 5:4–5).

Faith lies at the foundation of all courage, endurance, and insight. Because Paul believes, he speaks. Because he speaks, he gets stoned and dragged outside the city. And then he gets up, and because he believes, he goes on to speak again.

Where does this faith come from? According to Paul, faith comes by hearing, and hearing by the Word of God (Rom. 10:17). Whenever the Word is proclaimed, or the Scriptures read, in that moment faith is being formed in the believer's heart.

What is that Word? It is that Christ was crucified. He was buried in the tomb. On the third day, in accordance with the Scriptures, He rose again from the grave. A short time later, the Holy Spirit was poured out into the world with the express purpose of anointing that message, making it powerful to save. The gospel calls every kind of person. The one already a Christian is told to come. The one not a Christian is told to come. The nominal Christian, just a Christian on the surface of his life, is told to come. This is the gospel call. What does Isaiah say?

Look unto me, and be ye saved, all the ends of the earth;
for I am God, and there is none else. (Isa. 45:22)

What does the Lord Jesus say?

Come unto me, all ye that labor and are heavy laden,
and I will give you rest. (Matt. 11:28)

And what does the Spirit say, together with the bride?

Come. And let him that heareth say, Come. (Rev. 22:17)

And this is why we should always be ready to say, "Come, and welcome, to Jesus Christ." And for those who come, they should be assured that their afflictions will not disappear. But they should understand that when they come, their afflictions will start to make sense.

2 CORINTHIANS 5:1–6:2

CHRISTIANS IN THE JUDGMENT

As Christians, we must live our lives here in the light of the life to come. Those who live in the ways of YOLO are like pigs under a vast oak tree, looking for acorns. They do not consider what is above them, not at all, they do not care about the source of their blessings, not at all, and they keep their snouts pointing toward the dirt, always hunting for the next acorn. But we are summoned to a way of life that is completely and entirely different.

> For we know that if our earthly house of this tabernacle were dissolved, we have a building of God, an house not made with hands, eternal in the heavens. For in this we groan, earnestly desiring to be clothed upon with

our house which is from heaven: If so be that being clothed we shall not be found naked. For we that are in this tabernacle do groan, being burdened: not for that we would be unclothed, but clothed upon, that mortality might be swallowed up of life. Now he that hath wrought us for the selfsame thing is God, who also hath given unto us the earnest of the Spirit. Therefore we are always confident, knowing that, whilst we are at home in the body, we are absent from the Lord: (For we walk by faith, not by sight:) We are confident, I say, and willing rather to be absent from the body, and to be present with the Lord. Wherefore we labour, that, whether present or absent, we may be accepted of him. For we must all appear before the judgment seat of Christ; that every one may receive the things done in his body, according to that he hath done, whether it be good or bad. (2 Cor. 5:1–10)

Paul starts by comparing our mortal bodies to tents or tabernacles, which are to be replaced by an eternal body in the heavens, fashioned by God Himself (v. 1). Dwelling in these tents is a time for *groaning*, as we look for our permanent heavenly house, which will finally clothe us (v. 2). If we are clothed in this way, we will not be found naked (v. 3). While we live down here in these tent bodies, it is a burden, and so we groan under it. But we do not groan in the direction of "no body," but rather in the direction of "ultimate body," so that our mortal bodies might be swallowed up by life (v. 4). God has fashioned us for this very thing (v. 5a), and He has given us the earnest payment of His Spirit

(v. 5b). An earnest payment is a guarantee, meaning that if the promise is not fulfilled, the earnest payment is forfeited. This means that if a believer is lost and goes to Hell, the Spirit goes with him, which is absurd. All this means that the Spirit is dwelling here now, and He is *with* us in these tents. This is the ground of our confidence. We know that to be present in these bodies is to be absent from the Lord in Heaven (v. 6), which means we must walk by faith (faith generated by the Spirit), and not by sight (v. 7). Our confidence looks forward to the time when we leave this body and are present with the Lord (v. 8). This is why we work as hard as we do, so that whether we see Him with our eyes or not, we are nevertheless accepted by Him (v. 9). Absolutely every one of us is going to appear before the judgment seat of Christ, and we will all receive what we deserve according to our deeds in the body, whether good or bad (v. 10).

We learn from Scripture how the Spirit helps us to groan as we ought. When Paul points out we live in a tent, he says we *groan* (*stenazo*, v. 2). With the burden of tabernacling, we groan (same word, v. 4).

Paul teaches something very similar in Romans 8. The whole creation groans (*stenazo*) like a woman in labor (Rom. 8:22). We who have the firstfruits of the Spirit groan as we look forward to the redemption of our bodies (Rom. 8:23). So the groaning is aimed at the day of resurrection. Yearning toward that same end, the Spirit Himself labors with groans too deep for words (Rom. 8:26). This is because the entire cosmos is pregnant with the new creation. The creation groans for the day of resurrection. We believers groan for it. The Spirit helps us in our groaning. When we look at this, and experience this, our basic question ought always to be, "When's the due date?"

Putting all this together, we can see what happens when believers die. Our bodies are called tabernacles, and this is where we live now. If this tent is destroyed, we are (Paul says) "with the Lord." This is some sort of intermediate state, and too many Christians confuse this intermediate state with our final eternal state. That final eternal state is after the dead are raised. Being a ghostly spirit in Heaven is not our final hope. We are Christians, and this is why we believe in the resurrection of the *body*.

This leads us to the question of Christians and their relationship to the judgment to come. As we consider the end of the world, we must distinguish between two different aspects of how God will judge the world at the last day.

In the first instance, there is the Great White Throne Judgment. We see this in Revelation 20:11–15. This is a judgment that distinguishes and separates the saved from the lost. We see the same thing in Matthew 25, in the separation of sheep and goats (Matt. 25:31–36). Those who are saved through this judgment are saved on the sole basis of the righteousness of Jesus Christ, imputed to them by the grace of God. You will stand in this judgment, or not, on the basis of whether or not you are found in Christ. Salvation is based on whether or not our names are found written in the "book of life from the foundation of the world" (Rev. 17:8). The basic question here concerns your justification. Have you had the righteousness of Christ imputed to you, or not?

2 CORINTHIANS 5:1-6:2   57

But there is another judgment, often called the *Bema*-seat judgment. *Bema* is the word that is used for the judgment seat of Christ here in verse 10 of our passage. This is a judgment that evaluates the lives of Christians and rewards them (or not) on the basis of how they lived. This is an evaluation of our sanctification. Paul refers to this in our passage here, but also elsewhere.

> For we shall all stand before the judgment seat of Christ. . . . So then every one of us shall give account of himself to God. (Rom. 14:10, 12)

If we compete in accordance with the rules, we will be crowned (2 Tim. 2:5).

> And every man that striveth for the mastery is temperate in all things. Now they do it to obtain a corruptible crown; but we an incorruptible. (1 Cor. 9:25)

Now because of our justification, we know that the judgment that separates the sheep from the goats is a judgment that will declare us to be perfect. Perfect in Christ, but perfect, nonetheless. We have nothing to fear as we come to stand before God. And because we have nothing to fear, we can long for the day when God evaluates all our words, actions, thoughts, disputes, and snarls. Let us say you had a falling out with a friend. What this doctrine does is help you to yearn for the day when God will tell you whether you were right or wrong. And if you can't yearn for that day, this means that you already know that you were in the wrong.

As believers, we come to the *bema*-seat having already had the vindicating verdict pronounced over us. That verdict is "not guilty." That verdict is *no condemnation* (Rom. 8:1). And that is the foundation for everything else that we do.

NO CRAVEN, CRAWLING THING

The fear of God is not an attitude that flinches at the sound of God's name. In this passage, the fear of God is a driving motive force for evangelism, and evangelism is a proclamation of the good news, not the declaration of dreadful news. We therefore need to understand the fear of God as something that's powerful and attractive.

> Knowing therefore the terror of the Lord, we persuade men; but we are made manifest unto God; and I trust also are made manifest in your consciences. For we commend not ourselves again unto you, but give you occasion to glory on our behalf, that ye may have somewhat to answer them which glory in appearance, and not in heart. For whether we be beside ourselves, it is to God: or whether we be sober, it is for your cause. (2 Cor. 5:11–13)

In the light of this judgment, in light of the fact that every man will stand before the judgment seat of Christ, we know what it is to fear the Lord. Precisely because we know "the terror" of the Lord here, we seek to persuade men (v. 11). Persuade them of what? Persuade them to consider their true condition. A human life without true, complete, utter, and entire accountability has not yet been lived and never will be. It is madness not to factor this fact into how we live our lives. Consequently, Paul lives his life *coram Deo*, in the manifest sight of God, and Paul trusts that what he is doing is manifest enough to be obvious to the consciences of the Corinthians also.

The reason Paul is writing about this here is not to brag *to* the Corinthians, but rather to give them an opportunity to brag *about* him. They needed the material so that they could answer the false teachers at Corinth—identified by Paul here as those who glory in appearances, and not in the heart (v. 12). Paul acknowledges that some will think he is crazy, while others will call him sober-minded. He divides it up this way: "If we are out of our minds, it is for God. If we are calm and judicious, it is for you Corinthians" (v. 13).

There is a *sense* in which believers ought to care about our testimony and reputation. Elders should have a good reputation with outsiders, for example (1 Tim. 3:7). A good name is greatly to be valued (Prov. 22:1). Because we live lives of integrity, those who slander us should be ashamed of themselves (1 Pet. 2:15).

But at the same time, Jesus tells us that when all men speak well of us, we should consider that as a real danger sign (Luke 6:26). That is how they speak of false teachers. In our passage, Paul tells us that false teachers cultivate and pursue appearances (v. 12). This is their currency. They care about appearances, which is not the same as caring about testimony. Caring about testimony is caring about the *truth*, and caring about appearances is caring about the *lie*.

So test your hearts in this. Would you rather be truthful and thought a liar, or a liar and thought a truth-teller? Would you rather be courageous and thought a coward, or a coward who is thought to be courageous? Would you rather be honest and thought to be dishonest, or dishonest and thought to be honest? The answer will reveal whether you are standing before God or men.

What we should pursue is an attitude of jubilant terror. Knowing therefore the terror (*phobos*) of the Lord, we seek to persuade men. Again, the fear of God is not a craven thing. This is not a religion for lickspittles. Although the same word (*fear*) is used, there is a vast difference between the flinching that wants to avoid a blow and the awe that swallows you up when you consider that the paving stones in all God's palaces contain numberless galaxies. Perfect love casts out the first kind of fear (1 John 4:18), and perfect love ushers in the second kind (Ps. 8). What is *man*, that you are mindful of him?

This is why Paul can tell the Philippians to work out their salvation with *fear* and *trembling* (Phil. 2:12), then later tell them to rejoice *constantly* (Phil. 4:4). Rejoice with fear and trembling. This is what the kings of the earth are commanded to learn: "Serve the LORD with *fear*, and *rejoice* with *trembling*" (Ps. 2:11).

And when Moses and Aaron were dedicating the tabernacle, the fire of God flared out from the glory of God "and consumed upon the altar the burnt offering and the fat: which when all the people saw, *they shouted*, and fell on their faces" (Lev. 9:24). These were not religious feelies. In the next chapter, the fire of God devours Nadab and Abihu

(Lev. 10:2). The people fall on their faces, shouting and jubilant in their terror.

This is joy unspeakable and full of glory. And this is what the Scriptures point us to, constantly. Paul wants us to have the "spirit of wisdom and revelation in the knowledge of him." He wants us to have the "eyes of our understanding enlightened" so that we might "know what is the hope of his calling," not to mention the "riches of the glory of his inheritance in the saints." And what else? The "exceeding greatness of his power to us-ward who believe, according to the working of his mighty power" (Eph. 1:17–19).

Paul also prays that we might be "able to comprehend with all saints what is the breadth, and length, and depth, and height," and more than that, to "know the love of Christ, which passeth knowledge," and he wants us to be "filled with all the fulness of God." He wants us to ask and think *that* and then to commit it all to the one who can do "exceeding abundantly above all that we ask or think, according to the power that worketh in us" (Eph. 3:18–20). He wants us to grasp the ungraspable, and to know the unknowable, and to be filled with the infinite. And then he wants us to be hungry for more than *that*.

> Whom having not seen, ye love; in whom, though now ye see him not, yet believing, ye rejoice *with joy unspeakable and full of glory*. (1 Peter 1:8)

This is the reality that will make evangelism potent. Knowing what it is to fear the Lord, we seek to persuade men. As we reflect Christ, we point the way to Christ. And as we bear witness to Him, we pray for the fire to fall. We pray for the fear of God to fall, and we cannot expect it to fall on the world unless we are willing for it to fall on us.

THE STUPEFYING TRANSACTION

When the gospel is stated in its bare outlines, it is the kind of thing that takes the breath away. It leaves us stupefied. If we hear the preacher declaring the unvarnished truth, we look heavenward in amazement. *You can't be serious.* We look at the preacher closely to see if he is showing signs of running a fever. How can these things be? But in the cross, that moment of glorious exchange, an exchange of sin and righteousness, we see that the wisdom of God is terrifying in its mere goodness.

But when I say "exchange," or use the word "transaction," do not think for a moment that in salvation, God does His part, while we do ours. No. In the moment that counts, the entire transaction is conducted by God alone. This is all of grace.

> For the love of Christ constraineth us; because we thus judge, that if one died for all, then were all dead: And that he died for all, that they which live should not henceforth live unto themselves, but unto him which died for them, and rose again. Wherefore henceforth know we no man after the flesh: yea, though we have known Christ after the flesh, yet now henceforth know we him no more. Therefore if any man be in Christ, he is a new creature: old things are passed away; behold, all

things are become new. And all things are of God, who hath reconciled us to himself by Jesus Christ, and hath given to us the ministry of reconciliation; To wit, that God was in Christ, reconciling the world unto himself, not imputing their trespasses unto them; and hath committed unto us the word of reconciliation. Now then we are ambassadors for Christ, as though God did beseech you by us: we pray you in Christ's stead, be ye reconciled to God. For he hath made him to be sin for us, who knew no sin; that we might be made the righteousness of God in him.

We then, as workers together with him, beseech you also that ye receive not the grace of God in vain. (For he saith, I have heard thee in a time accepted, and in the day of salvation have I succoured thee: behold, now is the accepted time; behold, now is the day of salvation.) (2 Cor. 5:14–6:2)

We have settled upon this reality, which is that if one died for all, then all have died (v. 14). And so it is that we are bound by the love of Christ. And the reason He died for all was so that we could stop living toward ourselves, but rather toward the one who died for us and rose again (v. 15). This is why we don't look at *anyone* from an earthly vantage point alone anymore—we used to know Christ on that level, but no longer (v. 16). If someone is in Christ, absolutely everything is transformed—new for old (v. 17). This is a new world, a new creation. It is all from God, who reconciles us in Christ and then gives us the ministry of reconciliation (v. 18). That is, God was in Christ, reconciling the world to Himself, refusing to impute their trespasses to them, and giving us the charge to tell them that this is now the case (v. 19). So we are now ambassadors, as though God Himself were speaking through us: *"Be* reconciled to God" (v. 20).

And so we come to one of the weightiest verses in the entire Scriptures. God made the sinless one to be sin for us, so that He could reckon us, the sinful ones, to be the righteousness of God in Him (v. 21). This is the basis of our gospel appeal. As co-workers of God, we plead with sinners not to receive the grace of God in vain (6:1). Paul then states the invitation, using the words of the Septuagint, quoting Isaiah 49:8. God says that He has heard us in the time accepted and has comforted us in the day of salvation—and that day of salvation is *now* (v. 2). God always promises salvation today—we have no guaranteed tomorrow.

This means we must look at the entire world through new eyes. If we know the gospel, then we have to look at the whole world differently. Paul absolutely refused to look at anyone in the old way anymore, and this was because he could not look at Christ in the old way anymore—now that Christ had risen. C.S. Lewis once put his finger on the direct implication of this:

> It is a serious thing to live in a society of possible gods and goddesses, to remember that the dullest and most uninteresting person you talk to may one day be a creature which, if you saw it now, you would be strongly tempted to worship, or else a horror and a corruption such as you now meet, if at all, only in a nightmare. All

day long we are, in some degree, helping each other to
one or other of these destinations.[1]

When you are dealing with someone who is being
tedious, meditate on the glory that is coming for them and
that will inexorably swallow them up. How can you believe
that so-and-so is boring, or tedious, or annoying? Don't you
believe Christ *rose*? And remember, such an exercise is the
very best way for you to mortify the ways in which *you* are
being tedious.

So here is the ground of the appeal. Note that God objec-
tively reconciled the world to Himself through Christ. The
thing is done. We are therefore not pleading with the world
to get themselves reconciled to God. The plea is stronger
than that: "The world has *been* reconciled, and so therefore
be reconciled." To remain stiff-necked and rebellious is to
receive God's offered grace in vain (6:1). But the vanity is
on our end, not the Lord's. *His* purposes always come to
pass. His decree can never fall to the ground. We are saying
nothing against the fact that God's sovereign decree settles
the matter. But it is still a heartbreak when residents of a
reconciled world insist on their own damnation.

How does God accomplish this great salvation? This is an
audacious imputation. One died for all, and therefore all
were dead. To grasp this, we have to comprehend the true
nature of Christ's substitutionary death.

There are two kinds of substitution. One you see in a bas-
ketball game, where one player goes in for another, and that

1. C.S. Lewis, *The Weight of Glory and Other Addresses* (New York: Macmillan,
1949), 14–15.

second player goes to the bench. One in, and one out. That is one kind of substitution, and it is *not* the kind of substitution that Christ provides for us.

The second kind of substitution is covenantal or representative substitution. This happens when we elect a congressman, for example, and he goes to Washington to represent our interests. When he votes, we vote. When he is caught up in scandal, we are humiliated. When he does right, we are pleased and gratified. This is covenantal substitution, *covenantal* representation.

Christ died for all as the representative head of the new human race. Just as when Adam sinned, we sinned (because Adam was our federal, or covenantal, representative), so also when Christ died, we died. When He was buried, we were buried. When He rose, we rose. When He ascended, we ascended. Because of all this, all our sins were imputed to Him. Because of all this, all His righteousness was imputed to us.

So Christ was never a sinner (1 Pet. 2:22; Heb. 4:15; 7:26; 1 John. 3:5; cf. Rom. 5:19; 8:3; John 8:46), but He who knew no sin was made sin (through God's imputation of our sin to Him). He was never a sinner, but He was *made sin* and had the full experience of all our sins credited to His account, and, during the course of those three hours on the cross, He bore the brunt of God's holy wrath against that sin. This is why, I believe, the land was thrown into darkness, because no creature could look on how marred and twisted He had become. He had no form or comeliness that we should look on Him (Isa. 53:2). He was stricken, smitten, and afflicted (Isa. 53:4). And because of all of the diseased death that was reckoned to Him, it became possible for life to be reckoned in the opposite direction (v. 15)—for the righteousness of Christ to be imputed to us (v. 21). This is an *audacious* salvation.

But do not miss the invitation that follows. When should we act upon this truth? The answer is plain. We should act on it as soon as we hear about it. Look at the calendar. Is it *today*? Now is the moment then. Now is the day of salvation. Look to Christ, and Christ will look toward you. If you peer into the darkness where Christ writhed, nailed to a gibbet, then God in His grace and kindness will shine the light of all Christ's righteousness on you. Not only so, but He will shine that light full in your face. Rise, O sleeper, and Christ will shine on you (Eph. 5:14).

Think of it. Consider our sins. How many lies? How much cheating? How much corruption? How many murders? How much road rage? How much disobedience to parents? How many porn downloads? How much vanity? How much theft? How many acrimonious marriages? The weight of those sins is enormous. But it is still finite. And they were all placed on the shoulders of Christ as He sank down into death.

And He then rose from the dead for our justification. This means that the riches of His glorious grace and the grace of His unblemished righteousness, which are *infinite*, were placed on your shoulders. And what should you do with this? There is only one thing you may do with it, and you are commanded to do this. You are summoned to *believe it*. Look to Christ, and He is here for you in the gospel.

2 CORINTHIANS 6:3–7:1

A BLIZZARD OF TROUBLES

The early church father John Chrysostom once said that the apostle Paul had gone through a "blizzard of troubles." This passage is one of the places where we learn something of them. And if the truth be told, we are probably just learning about a fraction.

Paul's adversaries at Corinth had apparently been arguing that Paul could not be from God—look at how much trouble he was in, all the time. The man was a controversy magnet, and this was upsetting to that breed of Christian who always wants to stay well away from all controversy magnets. But Paul's reply to them was that his troubles did not negate his ministry. Rather, his long endurance through those troubles *confirmed* his ministry. His was the way of the cross.

69

Giving no offence in any thing, that the ministry be
not blamed: But in all things approving ourselves as
the ministers of God, in much patience, in afflictions,
in necessities, in distresses, In stripes, in imprisonments, in tumults, in labours, in watchings, in fastings; By pureness, by knowledge, by longsuffering,
by kindness, by the Holy Ghost, by love unfeigned, By
the word of truth, by the power of God, by the armour
of righteousness on the right hand and on the left, By
honour and dishonour, by evil report and good report:
as deceivers, and yet true; As unknown, and yet well
known; as dying, and, behold, we live; as chastened,
and not killed; As sorrowful, yet alway rejoicing; as
poor, yet making many rich; as having nothing, and yet
possessing all things.

O ye Corinthians, our mouth is open unto you, our
heart is enlarged. Ye are not straitened in us, but ye are
straitened in your own bowels. Now for a recompence
in the same, (I speak as unto my children,) be ye also
enlarged. (2 Cor. 6:3–13)

Paul's language here is that of high poetry. But the subject
of his poetry was how many times he had been "beat up."
First, he says he is careful not to give offense in anything
(v. 3). He is of course talking about *unnecessary* offense.
Paul has shown us his calling card, attesting to his authentic
apostolic ministry. As it turns out, his calling card is covered
with bruises.

In the original, there are twenty-eight descriptive com-
ments. As Kent Hughes points out in his commentary, the

first eighteen are prefaced with the word "in," the following three by the word "through," and the last seven by the word "as."[1] Not only so, the first round comes to us in triplets. First we see *general* troubles: afflictions, necessities, and distresses (v. 4). The second triplet is made up of troubles from *others*: stripes, imprisonments, and riots (v. 5a). Remember that Paul went through riotous tumults in Pisidian Antioch, Iconium, Lystra, Philippi, Thessalonica, Corinth, Ephesus, and Jerusalem (Acts 13:50; 14:5, 19; 16:22; 18:12; 19:23; 21:27). That man knew his riots. Finally, the last triplet of troubles might be called *self-sacrificial*: labors, watching, and fasting (v. 5b).

How could Paul endure all this? Next, Paul gives us a list of the inner graces that made it possible for him to maintain his steady equilibrium, despite all the commotion around him. In the middle of this list he mentions the Holy Spirit Himself by name. Paul does what he does *by* pureness, knowledge, patience, kindness, the Holy Spirit, and genuine love (v. 6). He does it *by* the word of truth, the power of God, and the armor of righteousness on the right and on the left (v. 7). The word "armor" here would be better rendered as "weapons"—weapons for the right hand and the left. He does what he does *by* honor and dishonor, *by* evil report and good (v. 8a).

For the last seven, Paul gives us a series of paradoxes, all of them ending on an upward note of triumph. *As* deceivers, but actually true (v. 8b). *As* unknown, but actually well known. *As* dying, and yet "look at us live." *As* punished, but

1. R. Kent Hughes, *2 Corinthians: Power in Weakness*, Preaching the Word (Wheaton, IL: Crossway, 2006), 131-137.

actually not killed (v. 9). *As* sorrowful, but always rejoicing, and *as* poor, while actually enriching many others, and *as* possessing nothing while at the same time owning everything in the world (v. 10).

Paul then speaks straight to the Corinthians—our mouth is open, he says, and our heart is enlarged (v. 11). They were not restricted because of Paul and company, but rather were constricted in their own attitudes (v. 12). The kink in the hose was in them, and not in Paul. Paul pleads with them as with his own children—be enlarged in heart, just as Paul was (v. 13). This is something we can imitate the apostle in.

There are those who believe the ministry to be an indoor job with no heavy lifting. There was an old Southern joke that said a hot sun and a slow mule had been responsible for many a call to the ministry. This has always been a lure. There were men in the first century who confounded gain with godliness (1 Tim. 6:5). And remember what Paul warned against just a few chapters before: "For we are not, as so many, peddling the word of God; but as of sincerity, but as from God, we speak in the sight of God in Christ" (2 Cor. 2:17, NKJV).

This means there is a certain measure of grace in controversy. When there is constant trouble, it disrupts *marketing*. It discourages *sales*. It makes it hard to be friends with the world, and it makes it difficult to monetize that friendship. That's why Demas had to leave Paul's company to take a new position (2 Tim. 4:10). One mark of authentic ministry is that all the tumult makes it hard to monetize anything.

Notice that biblical joy is a bedrock joy, and not a frothy bubblegum kind of joy. It is not *happy happy joy joy*. It is not some superficial sentiment. Paul says, "sorrowful, yet always rejoicing" (v. 10, NKJV). This indicates that when Paul tells us elsewhere to rejoice all the time (Phil. 4:4), he is not urging us into some kind of a masochistic glee. The soil in which blessings grow is the soil of difficulty. The mines in which the diamonds of grace are found are the mines of difficulty. The legacy of peace that we inherit comes from an ancestry of difficulty.

Underneath it all is the bedrock of joy. Sorrowful, yet always rejoicing.

Paul concludes this section by urging expansiveness of heart upon the Corinthians. He tells them that it is because of *his* largeness of heart that he is telling them about all the troubles he has gone through. His mouth is open because his heart is enormous. Earlier he spoke because he had believed (2 Cor. 4:13). Here he speaks because he *loves*. "I will run the way of thy commandments, when thou shalt enlarge my heart." (Ps. 119:32).

When King Solomon pleased the Lord by asking for wisdom instead of other baubles and trinkets, what did God do for him? "And God gave Solomon wisdom and understanding exceeding much, *and largeness of heart*, even as the sand that is on the sea shore" (1 Kings 4:29).

Fussers don't have this largeness of heart. They fuss right, and they fuss left. They fuss about their meals, they fuss about the traffic, they fuss about the sermons, they fuss about the lack of things to grumble about. Because this spirit of grumbling had taken root at Corinth, the saints there had fallen prey to certain agitators who wanted to circulate their complaints. So Paul opens his heart wide and pours *everything* out. And it is at that moment that he tells them the problem is in their own twisted, constricted hearts.

Open up, Paul says. Imitate me as I imitate Christ. Join me and my company of great hearts.

It sounds inspiring, but what is the cost? It means going and walking with Paul as he works through his blizzard of troubles. This is why many opt to continue to fuss along through their small troubles . . . because they don't want a life of joy through great troubles. But when you are in the joy of the Lord, whether troubles are great or small, you are where Christ is.

ABANDONING THE SONS OF BELIAL

Remember that the point of this epistle is for Paul to defend the authenticity of his ministry after a crisis in Corinth. There were three groups involved. First there were the false teachers, the agitators that stirred up the trouble. Then there were the saints in Corinth who had initially been swayed, but after Paul's severe letter, had come back to their loyalty to Paul. And finally there were the saints who were still rattled, who still had the wobbles. These are the ones who Paul beseeches to "enlarge their hearts." And in this passage, we get to Paul's basic "call to action." We have come to the thing that they must *do*.

> Be ye not unequally yoked together with unbelievers: for what fellowship hath righteousness with unrighteousness? and what communion hath light with darkness? And what concord hath Christ with Belial? or

what part hath he that believeth with an infidel? And what agreement hath the temple of God with idols? for ye are the temple of the living God; as God hath said, I will dwell in them, and walk in them; and I will be their God, and they shall be my people. Wherefore come out from among them, and be ye separate, saith the Lord, and touch not the unclean thing; and I will receive you. And will be a Father unto you, and ye shall be my sons and daughters, saith the Lord Almighty.

Having therefore these promises, dearly beloved, let us cleanse ourselves from all filthiness of the flesh and spirit, perfecting holiness in the fear of God. (2 Cor. 6:14–7:1)

Our first task here is some debris-clearing: there is an important misunderstanding to get out of the way. In this section, Paul famously says that we are not to be "unequally yoked together with unbelievers." This is regularly applied to marriages and/or business partnerships. While this is a legitimate application, it is not what the text is talking about, and we have to be careful not to lose the original meaning. When Paul tells Timothy to take a little wine for his stomach and frequent ailments (1 Tim. 5:23), he is not trying to refute teetotalism—that is a legitimate *application* (by extension) but not what Paul is talking about. It is the same kind of thing here.

Paul's intent here is to urge the remaining wobbly Corinthians to make a complete break from the false teachers (whom we will get to know much better in later chapters). For now it will serve to distinguish the wolves on the one hand from the sheep who have been mauled by wolves on the other. Paul is appealing here to the latter.

Paul starts with the principle: do not be in harness together with unbelievers (v. 14). He then gives the rationale in a series of contrasts. Is there fellowship between righteousness and unrighteousness (v. 14)? Communion between light and darkness (v. 14)? Concord between Christ and Belial (v. 15a)? Partnership between faith and infidelity (v. 15b)? Agreement between the temple of God and idols (v. 16a)?

These destructive false teachers want to set up their idols in the Corinthians, saints who were the temple of God (v. 16b). But idolatry of any sort, including what was being promoted here by the false teachers, falls under the condemnation of the Old Testament Scriptures. What looks like a solitary quotation from the Old Testament starting in verse 16 is actually a complicated mash-up of quotations from about six different places in the Old Testament. The first two are promises of close and intimate fellowship taken from Leviticus 26:11–12 and Ezekiel 37:27. Then comes the promise of adoption, and this is taken from four distinct places: 2 Samuel 7:14, Isaiah 52:11, Ezekiel 20:34, and Isaiah 43:6.

Overwhelmingly, the six cited passages are talking about Israel coming out of exile and returning to their land. The culmination is the promise that God will be our *Father*, and we will be *His sons and daughters*. The Corinthians were the heirs of spectacular promises and, as such, had an obligation to cleanse themselves from all filthiness of spirit and flesh, perfecting holiness in the fear of God (7:1). That is Paul's call: break with these sons of Belial.

We can tell that this is the import of this passage from the overall flow of the argument. Dealing with these false teachers is, after all, the theme of the entire letter. But we can also see it in Paul's use of a word like *Belial*. The word probably means *worthlessness* and is used throughout the Old Testament to refer to covenant losers. (See, for example, the following: Deuteronomy 13:13; Judges 19:22 and 20:13; 1 Samuel 1:16, 2:12, 10:27, 25:17, 25, and 30:22; 2 Samuel 20:1; 1 Kings 21:10, 13; 2 Chronicles 13:7.) We're talking about covenant members who are wicked louts. This is precisely the kind of person that Paul was dealing with at Corinth, and so he asks the rhetorical question—what possible fellowship can there be between Christ and Belial?

Paul is talking about the pressing need for more church splits. The "unbelievers" Paul is talking about are his adversaries within the church. These are false *brothers*. "Do not be yoked with" means do not pal around with, enable, encourage, or otherwise link yourselves to these people.

The driver of all such splits, however, needs to be *holiness*. If we pursue holiness in the fear of God, a lot of the separating will take care of itself. Paul is reminding the Corinthians of their identity in Christ. In Christ, what are they? They are the *righteousness* of God (2 Cor. 5:21). They have been made *light* (2 Cor. 4:6). In Christ, they are a *new creation* (2 Cor. 5:17). They are the *temple* of God (2 Cor. 6:16). The virtues of the Corinthians have no fellowship, communion, concord, part, or agreement with the corruptions offered by the sons of Belial. Those corruptions include unrighteousness, darkness, worthlessness, infidelity, and idolatry. Holiness of life will drive all such things away.

Satan has two basic strategies for attacking the church. He attacks it by persecutions from without, and he attacks it by corruptions from within. The latter has been his tactic of choice in the American church, and it has worked very well for him. The root of all such corruptions is unholiness, usually with a sexual component (2 Cor. 12:20–21). This is why vast swaths of the evangelical church collapsed almost overnight when the challenges of the COVID panic first appeared. Evangelicalism is seriously diseased.

And so the application today should be obvious. Separate from—do not have anything to do with, do not follow, do not fellowship with—the ministries of anyone who is woke or semi-woke, or who compromises on evolution, or who is effeminate, or who makes room for homosexuality as an identity, or who ordains women to be pastors, or who advances any form of critical theory, or who would otherwise invite this generation's Clown Car Review into the church. This list may seem like a disparate collection of random problems, but we must learn to connect the dots.

Later in this letter, Paul connects all kinds of problems to the corruption of lust.

> For I fear, lest, when I come, I shall not find you such as I would, and that I shall be found unto you such as ye would not: lest there be debates, envyings, wraths, strifes, backbitings, whisperings, swellings, tumults [*about all kinds of topics*]: And lest, when I come again, my God will humble me among you, and that I shall bewail many which have sinned already, and have not repented of the uncleanness and fornication and

lasciviousness which they have committed [*and he un-covers the root problem*]. (2 Cor. 12:20–21)

Tragically, this list of troubles is not limited to mainline liberal churches. Because we did not heed the warnings of the apostle, the evangelical movement is shot through with the cancers of this kind of unbelief. The evangelical church has failed to be salt and light, and consequently the West is disintegrating, and the savorless salt is being trampled on by men. But . . . never forget that we serve a God who raises the dead.

So we must not just turn away from these corruptions of sound doctrine. That is insufficient. We must also pursue holiness, pursue righteousness, pursue Christ. And as we all converge on Christ, we are converging on one another (1 John 1:7). And the standard is not just to be negatively stated, where we refuse to have anything more to do with sons of Belial. No, it also means growth in love of worship, hospitality, psalm-singing, Sabbath feasting, and the cultivation of true community. Not that any of these things can be pursued in their own right, but rather that such things are the natural overflow when we pursue Christ alone.

2 CORINTHIANS 7:2–16

ACTUAL GOOD GRIEF

There are three kinds of grief in this passage. The first is Paul's godly response to the pastoral meltdown at Corinth. Paul had been entirely "cast down" (v. 6). Then there is the godly sorrow and grief that follows after sin and that results in true repentance (v. 10a). But the third kind, the sorrow "of the world," leads only to death (v. 10b).

> Receive us; we have wronged no man, we have corrupted no man, we have defrauded no man. I speak not this to condemn you: for I have said before, that ye are in our hearts to die and live with you. Great is my boldness of speech toward you, great is my glorying of you: I am filled with comfort, I am exceeding joyful in all our tribulation.

For, when we were come into Macedonia, our flesh had no rest, but we were troubled on every side; without were fightings, within were fears. Nevertheless God, that comforteth those that are cast down, comforted us by the coming of Titus; And not by his coming only, but by the consolation wherewith he was comforted in you, when he told us your earnest desire, your mourning, your fervent mind toward me; so that I rejoiced the more. For though I made you sorry with a letter, I do not repent, though I did repent: for I perceive that the same epistle hath made you sorry, though it were but for a season. Now I rejoice, not that ye were made sorry, but that ye sorrowed to repentance: for ye were made sorry after a godly manner, that ye might receive damage by us in nothing. For godly sorrow worketh repentance to salvation not to be repented of: but the sorrow of the world worketh death. For behold this selfsame thing, that ye sorrowed after a godly sort, what carefulness it wrought in you, yea, what clearing of yourselves, yea, what indignation, yea, what fear, yea, what vehement desire, yea, what zeal, yea, what revenge! In all things ye have approved yourselves to be clear in this matter. Wherefore, though I wrote unto you, I did it not for his cause that had done the wrong, nor for his cause that suffered wrong, but that our care for you in the sight of God might appear unto you. Therefore we were comforted in your comfort: yea, and exceedingly the more joyed we for the joy of Titus, because his spirit was refreshed by you all. For if I have boasted any thing to him of you, I am not ashamed; but as we spake all things to you in truth, even so our boasting, which I made before Titus, is found a truth. And his inward affection is more abundant toward you, whilst he remembereth the obedience of you all, how with fear and trembling ye received him. I rejoice therefore that I have confidence in you in all things. (2 Cor. 7:2–16)

Paul's exhortation here for the Corinthians to "receive us" echoes his earlier exhortation for them to open or enlarge their hearts (v. 2a). Paul says he has wronged no one, corrupted no one, and defrauded no one (v. 2b). This is perhaps an indication of the nature of the charges that had been made against him. Paul is not trying to *condemn* the Corinthians who are still on the fence—with all his heart he wants to die and live with them (v. 3) He is bold in writing to them because he is overjoyed in them and filled with comfort (v. 4). We now learn about how torn up Paul was in Macedonia—fears within, quarrels without (v. 5). But he was comforted two ways: first by the coming of Titus (v. 6), and second by the news Titus brought (v. 7). Paul was greatly comforted to learn about the Corinthians' "earnest desire," their "mourning," and their "fervent mind toward" Paul (v. 7). Paul had made them sorry with his severe letter, but he did not regret it now (v. 8a). Nevertheless, he says there had been some moments where he did regret it. Perhaps right after he hit "send."

Their sorrow was just for a season (v. 8b); it was a fruitful sorrow, not a damaging sorrow (v. 9). For there are two kinds of sorrow and grief. One leads to repentance and salvation, and the other leads to death (v. 10). Paul then describes their godly sorrow, the components of which were diligence, an eagerness to clear themselves, indignation, fear, vehement desire, zeal, and vindication (v. 11). In all this, the Corinthians went above and beyond. Paul goes on to clarify that, in his severe letter, he was not aiming at the ringleader in the congregation who had caused the trouble, nor was he defending himself; instead, he was demonstrating his pastoral care for all of them (v. 12). This is why the news from Titus was so good (v. 13). When Paul had bragged about the Corinthians to Titus, his boast was simply the same kind of truth he used to speak to them. And they had not embarrassed him (v. 14), so now Titus is warmly attached to that congregation as well (v. 15). Note that this deep affection is not inconsistent with obedience, and fear, and *trembling* (v. 15). The whole episode has caused Paul to rejoice in all things (v. 16).

Remember, after the meltdown situation in Corinth, Paul had sent Titus to deal with it by means of a severe letter. Later, Paul came to Macedonia, expecting to find Titus there—but Titus had been delayed, and Macedonia was falling to pieces. Everywhere Paul turned he ran into conflict (v. 5).

Internally, Paul was beset with fears that all his work might come crashing down. This was a common concern of his—were all those floggings for *nothing* (Gal. 4:11; 1 Thess. 3:5; 2 Cor. 11:28–29)?

But when Titus came, God comforted Paul (v. 6). Titus was the instrument of comfort, and God was the agent. This expression of comfort is likely an allusion to Isaiah 49:13 in the Septuagint—where God brings eschatological comfort to His people. The coming of Titus was like *that*. Christ has a body in this world, and He works good for His people through that body. We are the hands and feet of Christ Himself in the world.

The repentance of the Corinthians before Titus had been a convulsive and dramatic one. They were not at all trying to preserve their dignity, to put things right without having to humble themselves. Remember that Paul mentions their obedience, their fear, and their *trembling*. This is a combination of a felt and very real authority with deep and open affection—the kind that Paul displays with his enlarged heart.

So the Corinthians' repentance could not be described as being in any way nonchalant. They were diligent, they worked to clear themselves, there was real indignation, they feared, they showed vehement desire, they displayed their zeal and their hunger for vindication.

This was *actual* good grief. Paul sharply distinguishes godly sorrow from worldly sorrow. The fact that you did something wrong and are sorry about it does not by itself mean anything. Suppose you did something that was pretty tawdry, and you are humiliated about it. Every time you think about it, your forehead gets hot. You sinned on Monday, and you are sorry on Tuesday. Come Friday, and you are still gnawing on your sorrow, like a dog with a bone. You are sorry yesterday, sorry today, and sorry tomorrow. At this rate, you are going to *die sorry*. That kind of sorrow is one of the things that needs to be repented of. You are trying to pay for your sin with sorrow, and it is an insulting and inadequate payment. It fails necessarily.

The godly sorrow that Paul describes "worketh repentance to salvation." That salvation, remember, is Christ. Godly sorrow leads you where? Godly sorrow leads straight to Christ. Godly sorrow leads you straight to the place of *no regrets* (v. 10).

This is how you distinguish the right kind of sorrow from the deathly kind. The right kind of sorrow brings closure and healing. The wrong kind of sorrow is an open, ongoing, festering wound.

The only way such a thing could ever be possible is if all our regrets, and all the sins that produce such regrets, are bundled up together and laid on the shoulders of Christ at the moment when He bowed His head and died.

2 CORINTHIANS 8:1–24

AN AQUIFER OF GENEROSITY

The grace of God is endless, and so when that grace is shed abroad in a finite world, the results frequently appear to have no visible means of support. We don't understand where it could all be coming from . . . but it comes to us nonetheless. God's grace brings a peace that passes understanding.

> Moreover, brethren, we do you to wit of the grace of God bestowed on the churches of Macedonia; How that in a great trial of affliction the abundance of their joy and their deep poverty abounded unto the riches of their liberality. For to their power, I bear record, yea, and beyond their power they were willing

of themselves; Praying us with much intreaty that we would receive the gift, and take upon us the fellowship of the ministering to the saints. And this they did, not as we hoped, but first gave their own selves to the Lord, and unto us by the will of God. Insomuch that we desired Titus, that as he had begun, so he would also finish in you the same grace also. Therefore, as ye abound in every thing, in faith, and utterance, and knowledge, and in all diligence, and in your love to us, see that ye abound in this grace also. (2 Cor. 8:1–7)

Paul wanted to make sure that the Corinthians knew about the particular nature of the grace that God poured out on the churches in Macedonia (v. 1). In the context of great affliction, their abundant joy and their extreme poverty combined to produce a most generous gift (v. 2). Paul testified that they willingly gave as much as they could and then gave even more (v. 3). As Chrysostom once pointed out, in this situation, the Macedonians did the begging, not Paul (v. 4). Not only did they give as Paul's band had hoped, but they did this in the right order. They donated themselves to God first and then to Paul's specific project, and all in the will of God (v. 5). Apparently, Titus was delivering this letter to the Macedonians also, and as he had reminded them of their pledge on his previous visit, Paul is now looking for him to complete the giving campaign (v. 6). Paul then makes his pitch. As the Corinthians abounded in numerous graces—faith, speech, knowledge, diligence, and love—so should they abound in this grace of giving monetarily as well (v. 7). The grace bestowed on the

Macedonian churches was a grace of *giving* (v. 1), and Paul is seeking to find the same kind of generosity welling up in the Corinthians.

Now there are different kinds of gifts. By "gifts," I include pretty much anything going *out*—time, money, wrapped-up presents, hospitality, and so on. Every church should want to develop a culture of generosity, and this is the kind of culture that has many manifestations. This means babysitting. It means unloading moving vans. It means rallying to meet someone's financial crisis. It means barn-raising events. It means welcoming the imposed discipline of birthdays and Christmastime. It means openhandedness.

Christmas is a season for giving, and so why not use that annual time for practice? Whenever you go into a season of shopping for gifts, you should take special care to make sure you understand what you are doing. A gift as seen from the outside can be one of three things. First, it can be a bribe. Second, it can be an extortion payment. And third, it can be a true gift. Two of them are most unfortunate, and the third is the genuine article. How can we tell the difference?

A bribe is given by a manipulator, or someone who wants somehow to game the system. He gives in order to get. He gives presents in order to get presents. He gives compliments in order to receive compliments. He donates to the church so that others will see him in that role. This was the sin of Ananias and Sapphira (Acts 5:1ff). Jesus warns against it sternly (Matt. 6:1).

An extortion payment is given by someone who is under duress. He gives in order to be left alone. Say a man gives a birthday present and breathes a sigh of relief because he doesn't have to think about *that* for another year. This is the sin that Paul is trying to teach us to avoid in the next chapter (2 Cor. 9:7).

A *true gift* is what the Macedonians offered here. They gave themselves first to God (v. 5) and then turned and gave to others. Christmas morning should be the second unwrapping of the gift. You give yourself to God first, and He unwraps you, and *then* you give your gift to the other person. A generous person gives in order to get, in order to be able to give some more. When we are generous, God promises to be generous to us. We therefore cultivate generosity in order to receive His generosity, but not because we are being grabby. We give in order to get, because that is how we are enabled to be even more generous. Our aspiration should be for this to become our way of life.

This pattern results in an aquifer of generosity. What is happening when this wonderful thing occurs? In this chain of events, God gives first. The word *charis* (grace, favor, benefit, or gift) is used eight times in chapters 8 and 9. God bestowed His grace on the Macedonians (v. 1), which is where their giving spirit first originated. And Paul wants to see the same thing start happening in Corinth (v. 7).

Remember that this was a one time special-need offering. We are not talking about the tithe here, or regular giving. This was a relief offering for the saints in Jerusalem. It was off-budget.

As the Macedonians gave to their fellow saints in this way, it created a bond of *koinonia*-fellowship (v. 4). The Sharing of goods is *fellowship*, just as the sharing of food is fellowship. We partake of one another when we give. We are intertwined when we give. When we give, we are being knit together.

For the Macedonians, this geyser of generosity came about in a unique set of circumstances. First, the grace of God came down upon them (v. 1), and then the providence of God surrounded them with a great trial of affliction (v. 2). In *that* setting, their deep poverty combined with their abundance of joy to erupt in an effusion of giving. The word for deep is *bathos*, which we get the word "bathysphere" from. Their poverty was down in the Mariana Trench—and when combined with heavenly joy, it surfaced into a remarkable gift.

Paul is going to develop this much more in the next two verses. When we give to others properly, we are doing so in the footsteps of the Lord Jesus. This is part of what it means to follow Him. Christ was rich, and He became poor as a gift, so that those who were poor might be made rich through Him (2 Cor. 8:9).

There is no generosity without Christ. The engine that drives the economy of generosity is not merchants, or manufacturers, or commercial interests, or anything like that. As we remember the gift of Christ, there will necessarily be a multitude of gifts following.

GET TO, NOT GOT TO

We are all active participants in this matter of giving and receiving, all the time, and so we must take care to cultivate the spirit of generosity. Like other virtues, this is not something that just happens all by itself. We must pay attention.

> I speak not by commandment, but by occasion of the
> forwardness of others, and to prove the sincerity of
> your love. For ye know the grace of our Lord Jesus
> Christ, that, though he was rich, yet for your sakes he
> became poor, that ye through his poverty might be rich.
> (2 Cor. 8:8–9)

Paul begins here by saying that he is not issuing a "commandment" (v. 8a). This is a stirring up of love, and not an exercise of raw authority. Paul is using the generosity of the Macedonians to stir up the Corinthians, just as he had earlier used the Corinthians to stir up the Macedonians (v. 24). He wants to test the sincerity of their love (v. 8b), a point that he repeats again in verse 24. And then Paul comes to the foundation of all true generosity. He begins by saying, "Ye know." Because they knew the gospel, the Corinthians already knew all about this. What did they know? They knew the *grace* of the Lord Jesus Christ (v. 9). And what did this grace entail? The eternal Word of God, infinitely wealthy, became bounded and finitely poor, and He did this so that we, through His poverty, might be made rich (v. 9).

Notice that Paul does not say that through the riches of Christ we are made rich. What makes us rich is the *poverty* of Christ, which means that before we share His wealth, we go through a *process*. We were wealthy in Eden, but we threw it all away, squandering it in the Fall. We became destitute, bankrupt, starving. Jesus Christ was born into *that* world, born of a woman, born under the law (Gal. 4:4). He shared our poverty, and as a consequence, we may share in

His wealth. But this *only works* because Christ is a federal or covenant representative—meaning, again, that He escorts us through a process. Divine wealth isn't just dropped on us.

The human race is fallen because the entire human race rebelled in the Garden of Eden. When our first parents sinned against God there, *the entire human race was present*. The entire human race acted, and when we acted, the whole race fell—even those individuals who had not yet been born.

When Adam disobeyed, we disobeyed in solidarity with him. When Adam ate the fruit, we ate the fruit in solidarity with him. When Adam fell into death-world, we fell into death-world also. Now all this means that the human race got into sin through covenantal solidarity, through our covenant head.

> Wherefore, as by one man sin entered into the world,
> and death by sin; and so death passed upon all men, for
> that all have sinned. (Rom. 5:12)

Now the way in is also the way out. If we got into sin by means of covenantal solidarity, we need to get out by means of covenantal solidarity. If the head of the human race plunged us into sin, then we need a new Head of the human race in order to get us out. And that is precisely what God provides for us in Christ. He is the second Adam (Rom. 5:14), the final and ultimate Adam.

> For as by one man's disobedience many were made sin-
> ners, so by the obedience of one shall many be made
> righteous. (Rom. 5:19)

> For as in Adam all die, even so in Christ shall all be
> made alive. (1 Cor. 15:22).

Jesus Christ is the friend of sinners. How did Christ share in our poverty? He was born into a fallen race to begin with. He was of the royal line of Judah, but the perks of that royalty were long since gone. He was not born into an aristocratic family. When He was dedicated at the temple, His parents offered up two turtle doves, the sacrificial option for *poor* people (Luke 2:24; cf. Lev. 12:8). And he began His earthly ministry with the baptism of John, which means that He began His ministry by identifying with sinners.

Everything that was assumed by Christ in the Incarnation was redeemed by Him in His death, burial, and resurrection. In the entire life of Christ (not just in His time on the cross) we see our redemption taking final and complete shape.

Remember what we saw in the first chapter:

> For all the promises of God in him are yea, and in him
> Amen, unto the glory of God by us. (2 Cor. 1:20)

Christ assumed a complete human life, an impoverished one, and He did so in order that everything He took on might be redeemed and glorified.

So when we come to give a gift, we must remember how Jesus gave, and how *much* He gave. "Ye know the grace of our Lord Jesus Christ." We should also look at the generosity of other Christians. If we just looked at Christ, we might be tempted to shrug apathetically and say, "I'm not

Jesus." But the Macedonians . . . they weren't Jesus either. Nevertheless, they still gave an amazing gift. Hebrews 10 tells us to "consider one another to provoke unto love and to good works" (Heb. 10:24). That is what Paul is doing here. When you are tempted to begrudge a need to give, then look around for some forgiven sinner like you, who has a much better set of excuses than you do, and who does not use those excuses.

Generosity proves the sincerity of your love. Do you love? Then love gives. Do you love? Then love sacrifices.

All of this is the path to a *get to, not got to* mentality. Giving is not an obligation, but rather a glorious opportunity. Look to Christ, always to Christ. Look to *your* "Macedonians." And last, look to your own heart, and if you are tempted to be discouraged by what you see there . . . look to Christ again.

A SNAKE-HANDLING CHURCH

When preachers take up the subject of money, it is too often the case that they focus on how the rank-and-file believers ought to be handling *their* money. But if we follow the lead of Scripture, and especially the example of Paul, we will find ourselves talking about how preachers ought to collect and handle money—and how they ought not to.

> And herein I give my advice: for this is expedient for you, who have begun before, not only to do, but also to be forward a year ago. Now therefore perform the doing of it; that as there was a readiness to will, so there

may be a performance also out of that which ye have. For if there be first a willing mind, it is accepted according to that a man hath, and not according to that he hath not. For I mean not that other men be eased, and ye burdened: But by an equality, that now at this time your abundance may be a supply for their want, that their abundance also may be a supply for your want: that there may be equality: As it is written, He that had gathered much had nothing over; and he that had gathered little had no lack.

But thanks be to God, which put the same earnest care into the heart of Titus for you. For indeed he accepted the exhortation; but being more forward, of his own accord he went unto you. And we have sent with him the brother, whose praise is in the gospel throughout all the churches; And not that only, but who was also chosen of the churches to travel with us with this grace, which is administered by us to the glory of the same Lord, and declaration of your ready mind: Avoiding this, that no man should blame us in this abundance which is administered by us: Providing for honest things, not only in the sight of the Lord, but also in the sight of men. And we have sent with them our brother, whom we have oftentimes proved diligent in many things, but now much more diligent, upon the great confidence which I have in you. Whether any do enquire of Titus, he is my partner and fellowhelper concerning you: or our brethren be enquired of, they are the messengers of the churches, and the glory of Christ. Wherefore shew ye to them, and before the

churches, the proof of your love, and of our boasting
on your behalf. (2 Cor. 8:10–24)

Against the background of "get to, not got to," which
we have already covered, Paul is now willing to give some
advice for the Corinthians on giving. They had indicated
a year before their eagerness to give (v. 10). So Paul says,
since you were willing a year ago, now would be a good time
to execute on that commitment (v. 11a). Paul wants them
to give from what they have (v. 11b), and he lays down the
principle: if there is a willing mind, God reckons the gift
according to the resources available (v. 12). Remember the
widow's mites (Mark 12:42).

But also recall how the Macedonians gave liberally out
of deep poverty (2 Cor. 8:1–2). Paul's intention is not to
burden the Corinthians in order to ease others (v. 13). The
principle is one of reciprocity—what goes around comes
around. He wants their current abundance to be a blessing
for the saints in Jerusalem, and another time it can run the
other way. This is what Paul means by equality (v. 14). He
then quotes Exodus 16:18, where in the gathering of the
manna there was always enough (v. 15).

Paul next returns to the eagerness of Titus to return
to Corinth (v. 16). Titus had been exhorted to go back
to Corinth, but he actually didn't require any persuasion
(v. 17). Paul then introduces two (unnamed) brothers.
The first is a famous brother (v. 18), of great reputation
among the churches and elected by them to escort the gift
to Jerusalem (v. 19). Some speculate that this was Luke.
The reason is so that everything might be above reproach

(v. 20), doing what is prudent and honest in the sight of both God and man (v. 21; Prov. 3:4). Paul then mentions a second unnamed man we might call the "earnest brother." Paul knew him, and apparently had selected him, but both men in verse 23 are called messengers (lit. *apostles*) of the churches, and so they both had an official status. Paul strongly commends all three men to the Corinthians (v. 23). They would be the ones carrying the gift. This passage then concludes with Paul exhorting the Corinthians to show these men the proof of their love and to vindicate his boasting on their behalf (v. 24).

There is an old warning for Christian leaders that cautions them about the three G's—glory, gold, and girls. This portion of 2 Corinthians is about the gold part. A story is told of a time when Thomas Aquinas called upon the pope and came in upon him when the pontiff was counting out a large sum of money. "You see," the pope said, "the church can no longer say, 'silver and gold have I none.'" Thomas replied, "True, holy Father, and neither can she now say, 'Rise up and walk.'" The point here is not that mammon is an idol out in the world—everyone knows that. The point is that mammon is a snare within the church, and it is particularly a snare for leaders *within* the church.

You cannot serve both God and mammon (Luke 16:13). We are told the Pharisees scorned Jesus for this teaching because they were lovers of money (Luke 16:14).

> For we are not, as so many, peddling the word of God; but as of sincerity, but as from God, we speak in the sight of God in Christ. (2 Cor. 2:17, NKJV)

I have coveted no man's silver, or gold, or apparel.
(Acts 20:33)

Christian elders must not be *covetous* (1 Tim. 3:3; 2 Tim. 3:2). When Paul thanks the Philippians, he is careful to let them know that his desire for them is not a grasping for money (Phil. 4:17). According to Peter, false teachers are cursed children, with hearts "exercised with *covetous* practices" (2 Pet. 2:14). "You who abhor idols, do you rob temples?" Paul asks (Rom. 2:22, NKJV). And there is a certain kind of teacher who supposes that godliness is a means of financial gain (1 Tim. 6:5). This is not a *rare* problem.

One of the abuses Paul had apparently been accused of by his adversaries at Corinth was the sin of fleecing the flock (see 12:14–18; 2:17; 7:2; 11:7–12). That is why he is at great pains to explain his financial precautions to the Corinthians here. And as the great apostle has set us a good example in this, let me take this opportunity to do the same thing.

In the history of our congregation here at Christ Church, we have never once passed the plate. The offering box is in the back, if you can find it. It is a practice I would recommend to all churches. We present the offering during worship, but we do not gather it then. After the second service the offering is counted, on the premises, by a team of men, not one man. When that offering is deposited in the bank by the church office, it is walked to the bank by a team of two staff members. The person who does our bookkeeping has no authority to cut checks. And so on. Now we do not do this because we are in a constant state of suspicion, squinting at one another with narrow eyes, but rather because—like Paul—we know that we live in a fallen world, and like Paul we want to do what is right in the sight of God and all men (v. 21). In all this, we are seeking to imitate the apostle Paul's approach to finances.

There are two kinds of idols. One kind of idol is simply a false god, a carved piece of wood or stone that you bow down to, light candles or leave baskets of fruit in front of, and so on. This kind of idol must simply be toppled, in the most literal sense. But there is another kind of idol, where a legitimate part of your life assumes an importance it ought not to have. In this case, repentance means restoring that person or thing to its proper role. For example, Paul teaches us that covetousness is idolatry (Eph. 5:5; Col. 3:5), but after repentance, a man must still handle money. He now needs to do it right, but he still needs to do it. A man must not love his wife more than Christ (Luke 14:26), but after he repents of her having been an idol, he learns to love her more than he ever did before (Eph. 5:25). That means he must learn how.

Some misguided brethren have thought that the promise of Mark 16:18 means that handling rattlers ought to be incorporated into the liturgy. Although we do not agree with that application, not at all, every church that takes an offering is a snake-handling church—which means all of them are. This is because Mammon is a snake. When deacons count out the offering after services, and all of them are spared, this is the goodness of God.

The only way it is possible for this to happen is by the grace of God found in Christ. And when this happens, it happens in such a way as to magnify, not the church where it happens, but rather the *reason* it happens. Notice the phrase Paul uses to describe the team of three men who were coming to collect the offering at Corinth. What does he call them? He calls them "the glory of Christ" (v. 23). And that is what a worship service is all about, the presentation of the offering included. The whole thing is calculated to glorify Christ.

Done right, the presentation of the offering is the glory of Christ. It is not a regrettable bit of business reality intruding into our spiritual time. The entire worship service—the music, the Scripture reading, the prayers, the preaching of the Word, and the placing of cash and checks on the same Table where the bread and wine are—needs to be aimed at this one thing. How can we best glorify and honor the Lord Jesus Christ? He is the one who died and rose, and we are the ones who are blessed in, through, and by His dying and rising. How could that not affect *everything*?

2 CORINTHIANS 9:1–15

THE GOD OF BOUNTIFUL HARVESTS

One of the great lessons we must learn is that God is far more generous than we are. Often, when we are confronted with scarcity, it is the result of our own greed, laziness, unbelief, and so on. When this starts to happen, we clutch at what we have even more, which perpetuates the downward cycle. God is the God of abundance, and the thing that corrupts the resultant affluence is something that we call *sin*.

> For as touching the ministering to the saints, it is superfluous for me to write to you: For I know the forwardness of your mind, for which I boast of you to them of Macedonia, that Achaia was ready a year ago; and

your zeal hath provoked very many. Yet have I sent the brethren, lest our boasting of you should be in vain in this behalf; that, as I said, ye may be ready: Lest haply if they of Macedonia come with me, and find you unprepared, we (that we say not, ye) should be ashamed in this same confident boasting. Therefore I thought it necessary to exhort the brethren, that they would go before unto you, and make up beforehand your bounty, whereof ye had notice before, that the same might be ready, as a matter of bounty, and not as of covetousness.

But this I say, He which soweth sparingly shall reap also sparingly; and he which soweth bountifully shall reap also bountifully. Every man according as he purposeth in his heart, so let him give; not grudgingly, or of necessity: for God loveth a cheerful giver. (2 Cor. 9:1–7)

Paul says that on one level it is unnecessary for him to again go over his teaching on finances and giving to the saints (v. 1). He knew they had covered that previously. They had been very eager to give the year before, and Paul had bragged on them to the Macedonians, which is part of the reason why *they* were provoked into zealous generosity (v. 2). But Paul had sent these brothers on ahead to make sure the gift was ready, because otherwise it would look like Paul had been boasting in vain (v. 3). The issue was not the donation itself, but rather whether the donation was prepared and ready to go (v. 4). Imagine the humiliation if the raggedy Macedonians showed up at Corinth with their big gift, and the well-to-do Corinthians had to say, "Oh, yeah, we said we would do that, didn't we?" So this is why Paul sent on the brothers mentioned in the pre-vious chapter. He knew that if the gift was unprepared, there would be a temptation to try to squeeze it out of the Corinthians, or to hurry it up, and that would be covetous-ness and not bounty (v. 5). The word rendered *bounty* in this section is literally *blessing*.

And so Paul now comes to the central principle: money is seed corn, and the amount of the harvest is directly cor-related to the amount that is sown (v. 6). Sow sparingly, reap sparingly—sow generously, reap generously. This is not just a matter of amounts, but also of *attitudes*. Each donor should settle the amount to be given in his own heart and then give that amount. *He* is responsible to monitor that—no grudging, no crisis giving. And why? Because God loves a cheerful giver (v. 7).

The thing that paralyzes us is our blind faith in the static and fixed nature of the created world. This leads to zero-sum thinking, which in turn leads to a grasping selfishness. Unlearning this zero-sum mentality is the hardest thing in the world—in order to do it, you have to mortify envy, lust, greed, and all the rest of that rancid crew.

Zero-sum thinking assumes that the size of the pie is necessarily fixed, and that more for someone else means less for you, and that more invested in the soil means less for you, and that more given to kingdom work means less for you. Because there is always the same amount of stuff, the thinking goes, the more other people have, the poorer we get. But this is wrong. God has placed us in a world where the pie is constantly growing. Envy stares malev-olently at the percentages, and not at the goodness of abundance. But what would you rather have? One percent of a million dollars, or fifty percent of fifty cents? One is smaller than fifty.

We have been taught to view everyone as *consumers*. But why not producers? We are born into this world with only one mouth and with two hands. Why shouldn't we produce twice as much as we consume?

> In a multitude of people is a king's honor, but in the lack
> of people is the downfall of a prince. (Prov. 14:28, NKJV)

Now one of the ways that grifters corrupt what Paul is teaching here is by doing their manipulative thing and then adding a note that says that God wants their victim to give cheerfully (*hilaros*). In other words, they disobey the assigned preconditions for creating generosity and then demand that the donor ignore the fact that they did so.

A similar thing happens when people invent draconian Sabbath restrictions that turn the joy of Sabbath rest into the equivalent of eating a bowl of driveway gravel—and then, when somebody protests the treatment, they lugubriously and solemnly inform them that God wants us to learn how to call the Sabbath a delight (Isa. 58:13). Yes, but delighting in the Lord's Sabbath is not the same thing as delighting in some people's idea of a Sabbath.

A demand for generosity—whether it's an emotional demand, an authoritative demand, or some other— quenches the desire to do any such thing. This principle applies in multiple areas. Nobody wants to pitch in to help out the dispensers of buzzkill. ("Why don't you kids visit us more?" The thought bubble over their heads says, "Because of conversations like this one.")

What is God like? Our God is a generous God. When He summons us to a life of generosity, He is not trying to squeeze riches from us to fill up His coffers. He doesn't need us in that way. "If I were hungry, I would not tell thee: for the world is mine, and the fulness thereof" (Psalm 50:12). He summons us to generosity so that we might become more like Him. His requirement that we learn to give is a form of giving to us.

> Therefore be imitators of God as dear children. (Eph. 5:1, NKJV)

> Thanks be to God for His indescribable gift! (2 Cor. 9:15, NKJV)

We worship the God of the open hand. And when we look at that open hand, what we see is a nail scar. Sacrificial giving is the way of the Christian because it was the way of Christ.

WHEN IT RAINS RIGHTEOUSNESS

God is seeking to grow us up into a particular kind of person, and He is going to provide us with whatever is necessary to accomplish His intention in that. God has no goals for us "in theory" that he hasn't also provided for. The *telos* of our lives is to be conformed to the image of Jesus Christ (Rom. 8:29; Phil. 3:21). The last day will not consist of us opening our spiritual ledger books in order that the number of commands kept and broken might be tallied up. Eventually we

will all become what we have been becoming, and God will
have provided you with what you needed along the way.

> And God is able to make all grace abound toward you;
> that ye, always having all sufficiency in all things, may
> abound to every good work: (As it is written, He hath
> dispersed abroad; he hath given to the poor: his righ-
> teousness remaineth for ever. Now he that ministereth
> seed to the sower both minister bread for your food,
> and multiply your seed sown, and increase the fruits of
> your righteousness;) Being enriched in every thing to
> all bountifulness, which causeth through us thanksgiv-
> ing to God. For the administration of this service not
> only supplieth the want of the saints, but is abundant
> also by many thanksgivings unto God; Whiles by the ex-
> periment of this ministration they glorify God for your
> professed subjection unto the gospel of Christ, and for
> your liberal distribution unto them, and unto all men;
> And by their prayer for you, which long after you for the
> exceeding grace of God in you. Thanks be unto God for
> his unspeakable gift. (2 Cor. 9:8–15)

God is fully capable of keeping us supplied. If He wants
us to drive somewhere, He will make sure we have the gas.
Hudson Taylor once put it well when he said that God's
work done in God's way will never lack for God's supply.
This is provision enough for *every* good work (v. 8).

Paul then gives us a chain of three quotations. The first
is from Psalm 112:9—the man who is generous to the poor
has a lasting *righteousness*. Then Paul quotes Isaiah 55:10,

virtually verbatim from the Septuagint, with Paul supplying the conclusion from Hosea 10:12—that God will multiply their seed and will also increase the fruits of their *righteousness* (v. 10). Great benefits will accrue from this. The first blessing is that there will be thanksgiving rendered to God (v. 11). Not only are the saints blessed, but God is *thanked* (v. 12). That's good. The second great blessing is that God is *glorified*—submission to the gospel by Christians and liberal giving in all directions brings glory to God (v. 13). That's good also. The third great blessing is the growth of mutual affection between believers (v. 14). Remember, too, that this gift is bridging a Gentile/Jew divide. Possessors of grace are drawn to others in whom that same kind of grace dwells. And Paul concludes by rendering thanks to the giving God, the God who has tendered to us the unspeakable gift (v. 15).

Too often we think of righteousness in terms of integrity and uprightness and keeping the law. This, we assume, is in some sort of tension with mercy. But in the ways of God, in the pattern of gospel, we find something different. "Mercy and truth are met together; righteousness and peace have kissed each other" (Ps. 85:10).

The man who gives to the poor—his *righteousness* endures forever (Ps. 112:9). And when God multiplies the seed of generosity, it is so that the harvest of *righteousness* might be abundant.

> Sow to yourselves in righteousness, reap in mercy; break up your fallow ground: for it is time to seek the LORD, till he come and rain righteousness upon you. (Hos. 10:12)

Sow righteousness, reap mercy. Sow mercy, reap righteousness. Plant the right crop in the right soil, and God will ensure that it *rains* righteousness. Ultimately it is all the same crop, which means we are not wrong if we look for it to rain mercy as well.

God's provision will always leave room for generosity. The scales may vary—one saint in a prison cell may share a crust of bread, and great men of war may share honor and food with their brothers—as happened when David was made king.

> All these men of war, that could keep rank, came with a perfect heart to Hebron, to make David king over all Israel: and all the rest also of Israel were of one heart to make David king. And there they were with David three days, eating and drinking: *for their brethren had prepared for them.* Moreover they that were nigh them, even unto Issachar and Zebulun and Naphtali, brought bread on asses, and on camels, and on mules, and on oxen, and meat, meal, cakes of figs, and bunches of raisins, and wine, and oil, and oxen, and sheep abundantly: for there was joy in Israel. (1 Chron. 12:38–40)

You are God's workmanship, created in Christ Jesus to do good works, which God prepared and ordained beforehand for you to do (Eph. 2:10). Young men are to show a pattern of good works (Titus 2:7), and all of us are to be zealous after good works (Titus 2:14). Tabitha was a woman "full of good works" (Acts 9:36). Now here is the thing. *Good works cost both time and money.* So if God has assigned these good works to you, and God is Himself generous, do you think He will let you run dry in the middle of your tasks? Not a bit of it.

This word rendered here as *unspeakable* was apparently a word coined by the apostle Paul himself. This is the first appearance of the word anywhere in Greek. What is this indescribable gift? God gives us the gift of Himself. A virtuous man might venture to lay his life down for a righteous or a good man, "but God commendeth his love toward us, in that, while we were yet sinners, Christ died for us" (Rom. 5:8).

Notice the logic of Paul's argument: "For if, when we were enemies, we were reconciled to God by the death of his Son, *much more*, being reconciled, we shall be saved by his life" (Rom. 5:10). Since God has given us the gift beyond all possible gifts—the death, burial, and resurrection of His Son— what on earth could make us think that He might suddenly pivot and become stingy? Is God a cosmic scrooge? Is the right hand of the Almighty clenched? The idea of anything like that could make a cat laugh.

2 CORINTHIANS 10:1–18

WHEN FALSE TEACHERS STRUT

As we come to chapter 10 of this epistle, we need to be reminded again of who the players are. We have the majority of the Corinthian church, and they are on Paul's side—even though a number of them had just recently been brought *back* to Paul's side by means of his "severe letter."

In the opposite corner are the false teachers, who had instigated the rebellion in the first place. And then we likely have to budget for regular members of the church who were more entangled by the false teachers than others had been and who are still not reconciled to Paul.

The first nine chapters of this letter were directed to those on Paul's side. Now here in chapter 10, Paul moves to the necessity of church discipline. Something had to be done about those who were continuing to disrupt the unity of the congregation. It was now time to discipline those who refused to repent of their stubborn opposition. The time for talking was over.

> Now I Paul myself beseech you by the meekness and gentleness of Christ, who in presence am base among you, but being absent am bold toward you: But I beseech you, that I may not be bold when I am present with that confidence, wherewith I think to be bold against some, which think of us as if we walked according to the flesh. For though we walk in the flesh, we do not war after the flesh: (For the weapons of our warfare are not carnal, but mighty through God to the pulling down of strong holds;) Casting down imaginations, and every high thing that exalteth itself against the knowledge of God, and bringing into captivity every thought to the obedience of Christ; And having in a readiness to revenge all disobedience, when your obedience is fulfilled. (2 Cor. 10:1–6)

Paul begins with a deeply ironic statement. He knows that his enemies say that he is no great shakes in his public speaking, and he acknowledges that this is true—but only in part. He pleads by the meekness and gentleness of Christ, knowing that he, an unpolished speaker, could still write a very tough letter (v. 1). In addition, while there in person, he had been holding back, and the next time, he wouldn't be holding back. In verse 2, he essentially says, "Don't make me come down there." He pleads with them to make any personal boldness from him unnecessary. Because if *that* happens, he is going to unload on those who maintain that Paul walks "according to the flesh." He acknowledges that he has a physical body, but he doesn't fight that way; he does not war "after the flesh" (v. 3). His weapons are not carnal and earthly, but rather mighty through God in the toppling of citadels (v. 4). He has the ability to throw down "imaginations," to throw down any high pride that is anti-God, and to take "every thought" as the prisoner of Christ (v. 5). And verse 6 makes it plain that he is talking about doing *all of this* at the upcoming congregational meeting. As the Corinthian church submits, he will discipline any remaining outliers.

When we are studying Scripture, we must understand the difference between exegesis (what the original readers understood by it) and application (what we intend to do with it). There should be a great deal of overlap between the two, but they do not map on to one another perfectly. Here's an example we've looked at before. When Paul tells Timothy to take a little wine for his stomach and frequent ailments (1 Tim. 5:23), exegesis tells us that Timothy had frequent digestive ailments and that Paul told him that wine should help. One application could be a modern Christian taking a little wine for his stomach trouble, which would be a great deal of overlap. But another application could be to quote this verse in a debate with a teetotaler. This would be a legitimate application, even if Paul had never even imagined the *existence* of teetotalers.

We should learn this distinction because Paul's language here in this passage is high rhetoric indeed and, hence, can easily be applied to the cosmic forces of unbelief—Darwinism, postmodernism, atheism, relativism, and the universities that house them. And because we do encounter imaginations there, and high unbelief, and disobedience to Christ, all such are legitimate applications. This local problem at Corinth and these massive worldwide lies all grow from the same root, which makes such applications compelling. But the exegesis requires us to apply this language in the first place to a looming showdown with false teachers at Corinth. Paul was talking about a congregational meeting, the minutes of which would make pretty exciting reading.

Although going large is a legitimate application, we still need to beware. It is always easier to do battle with *isms* than with people. It is easier to refute Darwinism in a classroom than it is to fire a staff member for his belief in theistic evolution. Paul was preparing for battle with people who had names, and faces, and mothers, and sisters. And friends in the congregation.

The question is what to do when false teachers strut. In the Greek world, any rhetorician worth his salt would be anything but humble. Humility was for them a disqualification. But Paul was following Christ, who was gentle and lowly of heart (Matt. 11:29), and this meant that his humility was one of his *qualifications*. The "some" of verse 2 are most likely the false apostles of 2 Corinthians 11:5, 13–15. Their carriage was magnificent, and their ability to command large *honoraria* was significant. Their spirit was measured by the size of the speaking fee they could draw down.

Some things really haven't changed. If you read about somebody who can charge 25k for one talk, you can assume that they are important. But this metric, Paul says, is carnal. His opponents were trained in public speaking, and were both confident and charismatic. They were polished, and knew just when to slap the thigh. They were splashy, and knew how to put on a show. But Paul answers them with *gospel*—straight, no chaser (2 Cor. 4:2–6).

The humility and weakness that were characteristic of Paul's ministry are the kind of humility and weakness that will conquer the world. Blessed are the meek . . . for what? For they will *inherit the earth* (Ps. 37:11; Matt. 5:5). The foundation of this great spiritual cathedral will be anchored to the cornerstone of our Lord having been nailed naked to a pole and there suffering the indignity of a criminal's death. There was no doubt dried spittle still on His face. *That* is how God glorified the name of Christ and, by so, doing glorified His own name (John 12:28).

Satan had shown the Lord the kingdoms of this world, and all their glory (Matt. 4:8), and the Lord turned away from it. He was not turning away from glory—He was turning away from that *kind* of petty glory. He was rejecting a Tinseltown glory. He was refusing the thin glory of gold foil. He was turning down the superficial honor that came so easily to superficial apostles.

It is so easy for us to slip back into the respectable mentality that made these false apostles so attractive to *Christians*. The cross was one of the most excruciating instruments of torture ever devised, and we make it into silver jewelry. Such jewelry is fine, so long as we don't forget what it means. It is like wearing a delicate silver hangman's noose. Or an electric chair, wrought in fine gold.

A cross on the steeple is a fine thing to have, but it should not be treated as a brand or as a logo. And there are many hymns that sentimentally refer to Calvary. But that name comes from the Latin word for skull, *calvarium*—because, in English, our Lord died on Skull Hill. Golgotha is the Aramaic name for the same thing, so no refuge for us there. And the glory is that the cross of the Lord Jesus was the tent peg of God, driven into Sisera's head.

Our salvation was not accomplished by some delicate means.

A YARDSTICK IN THE MIRROR

The fundamental difference between Paul and the false apostles is that he was surrendered to a standard from outside the world, and they were submitted to a standard from within themselves. And when I use a word like *standard*, I am referring to both law and gospel. What is the standard for evaluating appropriate behavior? And what is the standard for telling men how they might be saved? Both law and gospel, in order to *be* law and gospel, have to be *extra nos*, from outside of us.

> Do ye look on things after the outward appearance? If any man trust to himself that he is Christ's, let him of himself think this again, that, as he is Christ's, even so are we Christ's. For though I should boast somewhat more of our authority, which the Lord hath given us for edification, and not for your destruction, I should not be ashamed: That I may not seem as if I would terrify you

by letters. For his letters, say they, are weighty and powerful; but his bodily presence is weak, and his speech contemptible. Let such an one think this, that, such as we are in word by letters when we are absent, such will we be also in deed when we are present.

For we dare not make ourselves of the number, or compare ourselves with some that commend themselves: but they measuring themselves by themselves, and comparing themselves among themselves, are not wise. But we will not boast of things without our measure, but according to the measure of the rule which God hath distributed to us, a measure to reach even unto you. For we stretch not ourselves beyond our measure, as though we reached not unto you: for we are come as far as to you also in preaching the gospel of Christ: Not boasting of things without our measure, that is, of other men's labours; but having hope, when your faith is increased, that we shall be enlarged by you according to our rule abundantly, to preach the gospel in the regions beyond you, and not to boast in another man's line of things made ready to our hand. But he that glorieth, let him glory in the Lord. For not he that commendeth himself is approved, but whom the Lord commendeth. (2 Cor. 10:7–18)

Paul is preparing to mount an attack on these apostles of the superficial. If any of these men think they belong to Christ, Paul also does (v. 7). Paul is gearing up for some ironical boasting in the next chapter, and here he says that if he were to boast of his authority, he would not be ashamed. And why? Because his authority *gave* and did not *grab* (v. 8).

The point was not to be a literary terrorist (v. 9). Paul is here referring to the charge that he writes a hot letter, while his pulpit presence is weak, and his eloquence is well beneath the standard (v. 10). Paul has already indicated this next point, but he says it again: on the next visit, his letters and his actions will *match* (v. 11). Paul has a standard outside himself. Those who check the length of their yardstick with another yardstick are not wise (v. 12). Even worse are the people who check their yardstick by holding it up to a mirror. Paul says that he uses the measure granted by God to him, and to them as well (v. 13). Paul is not straying outside his lane by dealing with the Corinthians, because he was the one who had first shared the gospel with them (v. 14). Paul refuses to encroach on another man's ministry but is of course open to mutual edification (v. 15). He is certainly open to having the Corinthians help him in the task of preaching the gospel in regions beyond them (v. 16). The one who glories should do so in the Lord (v. 17). Self-congratulation establishes nothing—only God's commendation counts for anything (v. 18).

We live in a subjective age, and so many people are not ashamed to say that their standard is provided by the guidance of their own heart. But the Scriptures reject this as truly foolish: "He that trusteth in his own heart is a fool: but whoso walketh wisely, he shall be delivered" (Prov. 28:26).

There are two kinds of fools. There are those who trust in their own hearts and say that this is what they are in fact doing. Here the folly is out in the middle of the table.

The second kind is the one who trusts in his own subjective understanding but clothes it in the more orthodox language of objective truth. We can see this in the parable that
Jesus told about the conceited Pharisee who went down to
the temple to pray. Jesus spoke the parable against those
who "trusted in themselves" (Luke 18:9). But the language
the Pharisee used was good, solid Reformed stuff. "God, I
thank *thee*, that I am not as other men are . . ." (Luke 18:11).
"Lord, all the credit for me being so wonderful goes to You,
and only to You." Something is still off. And beware: how
many of us have read that parable and thanked God that we
are not like that Pharisee?

In this passage, Paul is *genuinely* submitting the whole
thing to God. When we pray, we should talk like we mean it.

One of the best ways to tell if you are using a subjective
personal metric or an objective biblical metric is to ask
whether or not there is any possible scenario where you
would receive correction. How good are you at removing
the beam from your own eye (Matt. 7:1–5)? How good are
you at considering yourself, lest you also be tempted (Gal.
6:1)? How good are you at not judging others with a standard that would also flunk you (Rom. 2:1–3)?

Suppose the existence of an invisible recording device
hung around every neck that only recorded moral judg-
ments leveled against others. "She ought not . . ." "I can't
believe he . . ." "Those people are awful . . ." "Did you see
what . . ." Suppose God distilled an ethical code from all
of those statements and then judged each person in strict
accordance with *that* standard. All of us would be con-
demned. We would be in the position of David talking to

Nathan about Bathsheba, well before David knew they were talking about Bathsheba.

By way of contrast, we know that Paul was the real deal because of statements like this.

> For I know nothing by myself; *yet am I not hereby justified*: but he that judgeth me is the Lord. Therefore judge nothing before the time, until the Lord come, who both will bring to light the hidden things of darkness, and will make manifest the counsels of the hearts: and then shall every man have praise of God. (1 Cor. 4:4–5)

We then come to "boasting in the Lord." Here is a matter that requires real spiritual wisdom. The occasions for boasting in the Lord will arise when people think that *you* had something to do with whatever the blessing might happen to be. For example, God has been very good to us here in this Moscow project, and there is no way to talk about it without referring to it. But I still wince inside whenever I hear it referred to in a casual way. I even feel the same when I have to talk about it. And why? Because we must always be careful to boast in the Lord.

But we have to come to grips with the fact that thanksgiving must be expressed for *concrete* blessings. We cannot boast in the Lord, who dwells in the highest heaven, and who does nothing in particular. It is not boasting in the Lord to talk about the attributes of God in a way that is detached from all human history. God reveals Himself in His great and wonderful works. Miriam was not dancing beside the sea because she had just finished reading a chapter in a theological tome on the divine aseity. She was dancing because Jehovah had bared His strong right arm, and, as the song puts it, "Pharaoh's army got drownded."

And when we ask what this external objective standard is, we must immediately correct ourselves. The question is not what the standard is, but rather *who* the standard is. And the answer to that question is the Lord Jesus Christ, crucified and risen. The central message from Christ is not "Go over there and do those good deeds. Make sure your motives stay right." The central message is "Come, follow me." Of course we are to be given over to good works—but it is crucial that we do them while following Jesus, and not while standing up on a stage, trying to impress Jesus.

2 CORINTHIANS 11:1–33

BRIGHT ANGELS OF DARKNESS

The situation needed to be pretty dire in order to get Paul to talk about himself in a boastful way (even if the boasting was sarcastic), and we start to see in this passage just how dire it was. The Corinthians had been infiltrated by emissaries of Satan, the Lord of Lies himself, and some of the believers there were still under the influence of those lies.

> Would to God ye could bear with me a little in my fol-
> ly: and indeed bear with me. For I am jealous over you
> with godly jealousy: for I have espoused you to one
> husband, that I may present you as a chaste virgin to
> Christ. But I fear, lest by any means, as the serpent

beguiled Eve through his subtilty, so your minds should be corrupted from the simplicity that is in Christ. For if he that cometh preacheth another Jesus, whom we have not preached, or if ye receive another spirit, which ye have not received, or another gospel, which ye have not accepted, ye might well bear with him. For I suppose I was not a whit behind the very chiefest apostles. But though I be rude in speech, yet not in knowledge; but we have been throughly made manifest among you in all things.

Have I committed an offence in abasing myself that ye might be exalted, because I have preached to you the gospel of God freely? I robbed other churches, taking wages of them, to do you service. And when I was present with you, and wanted, I was chargeable to no man: for that which was lacking to me the brethren which came from Macedonia supplied: and in all things I have kept myself from being burdensome unto you, and so will I keep myself. As the truth of Christ is in me, no man shall stop me of this boasting in the regions of Achaia. Wherefore? because I love you not? God knoweth. But what I do, that I will do, that I may cut off occasion from them which desire occasion; that wherein they glory, they may be found even as we. For such are false apostles, deceitful workers, transforming themselves into the apostles of Christ. And no marvel; for Satan himself is transformed into an angel of light. Therefore it is no great thing if his ministers also be transformed as the ministers of righteousness; whose end shall be according to their works. (2 Cor. 11:1–15)

So Paul is going to boast, knowing it to be folly, and he wants the Corinthians to bear with him in it (v. 1). The reason this approach is justified is because of Paul's godly jealousy over their spiritual chastity (v. 2)—he wants them to be kept pure for Christ. His concern is that, as Eve was beguiled by the serpent through nuance, they, too, may have been corrupted and turned away from the simplicity found in Christ (v. 3). He then moves into sarcasm. If someone showed up with a different Jesus, or a different Spirit, or a different gospel, the Corinthians put up with it readily enough (v. 4). The false apostles' problem was their lying; the Corinthians' problem was putting up with their lying. Paul goes on to say that he does not believe himself to be inferior to any of these (false) super-apostles (v. 5). Though he was unpolished in speech, his knowledge was just fine— as the Corinthians well knew (v. 6). But if they knew that, then why did they start to doubt him? Did Paul wreck his testimony with them by charging them no money (v. 7)? Other churches supported him to minister at Corinth (v. 8). Was *that* the problem? Was he treating them as some kind of a charity case? When he was present there in Achaia, the Macedonians supported him (v. 9). He swears by the truth of Christ, that nobody is going to be able to stop this boast of his in Achaia (v. 10).

Is this because he doesn't love the Corinthians? God knows the answer to *that* (v. 11). Paul will continue to do this in order to undercut the boast of the false apostles, who were trying to claim that they worked on the same terms as Paul (v. 12). These men are false apostles, deceitful laborers, dressing up as apostles of Christ (v. 13)—and this is no wonder, because Satan himself appears as an angel of light (v. 14). Consequently, it is no big deal when Satan's ministers wear the livery or uniform of ministers of righteousness (v. 15a). Of course they would. But their end will be according to their actual works, not their pretended works (v. 15b).

We must not proceed on the basis of misleading caricatures. We should not picture the devil with horns and a pitchfork. We wrestle against the prince of the power of the air, and not against a cartoon villain. When the Lord Jesus was tempted by the devil himself, the devil showed Him all the kingdoms of men *and their glory* (Matt. 4:8). Put another way, Jesus was tempted to become a Satan-worshiper—but not the kind that plays around with severed goat heads, pentagrams, candles, and spells. The temptation had to do with cathedrals, moon landings, skyscrapers on Wall Street, fleets, armies, and empires.

Paul says in this passage that Satan looks like the opposite of what he actually is. It therefore follows that his ministers look the same—shiny and bright on the outside, and inside filled with bones and rotting flesh. Nobody will knock on your front door with some grotesque literature and say, "Hello. I am here representing the prince of darkness and have come to lead you astray." We must always beware the allure of self-righteous *respectability*. Paul requires Christian leaders to be respectable (1 Tim. 3:2), but we also need Christian leaders who know and understand that there is spiritual death in respectability of a certain kind. We should remember that Jesus taught that certain people couldn't believe in Him because they received honor from one another (John. 5:44). A certain kind of honor is carnal. The telltale sign is that the devil will always want to remove the offense of the cross.

On a slightly different note, we are taught in multiple places in Scripture that a laborer is worthy of his hire and that men who make their vocation from the proclamation of the gospel have every right to expect to be supported from that work. But, as we learn here, ministers also have the right, for tactical and strategic reasons, for reasons of the testimony, to refuse to take any money from people they are *currently* ministering to. This is particularly important for itinerant ministry. You can see the pattern here. Paul says that he was supported by the Macedonians in order to minister at Corinth (2 Cor. 11:9), and he would be more than happy to receive the support of the Corinthians when he began ministering in the regions beyond them (2 Cor. 10:15–16). This was not morally necessary, but it was *tactically* necessary. And why? Because there were liars on the loose.

When a ministry is not itinerant but is well-established such that the congregation supports its own ministers, other protections become necessary—honoring the same principles. It should be clear at a glance that there is no funny business with the money.

When it comes to faithfulness and loyalty, life is pretty straightforward. If we maintain the kind of godly jealousy that Paul exhibits here, we are enabled by the grace of God to keep it that way.

Paul compares Christians being lured away from the simplicity of Christ to the temptation that our first mother was enticed by. That temptation began with little shadings, little blurrings. The serpent asked, "Did God really say you couldn't eat from *any* tree in the garden?" (Gen. 3:1). In her reply, Eve said that they weren't even to *touch* it, which was her addition (Gen. 3:3). Then the serpent came up to his direct challenge: "You will not surely die" (Gen. 3:4, NKJV). What begins with a small lie can end with a great fall.

What is the simplicity of Christ that we preach?

The message is straightforward. We preach the person and the work of the Lord Jesus Christ. We declare who He was—the very Son of God—and we declare what He did: He took our sins upon Himself, endured the wrath of God for them, and sank down into death. Three days later, He came back from the grave, having left all of our sins behind Him, those sins remaining in death forever.

SPEAKING AS A FOOL

In the following verses, Paul asks us to excuse him while he speaks as a fool, and even then he keeps breaking voice to remind us that he is being sarcastic—because he *really* doesn't want us to think that he is actually taking any glory for himself.

There are parallel lines of boasting here. First, Paul indicates that he is fully able to meet the false apostles on their own ground. But second, he itemizes all the ways in which he trounces them with accomplishments that they never aspired to at all—to their shame. He sets his resume on the table before them, and they are astonished to note that it records all his arrests. "As many as desire to make a fair shew in the flesh, they constrain you to be circumcised; only lest they should suffer persecution for the cross of Christ" (Gal. 6:12). This is the motivation that lies beneath these alternative approaches to ministry. Winsomeness is a defense mechanism.

> I say again, Let no man think me a fool; if otherwise, yet as a fool receive me, that I may boast myself a little. That which I speak, I speak it not after the Lord, but as it were foolishly, in this confidence of boasting. Seeing that many glory after the flesh, I will glory also. For ye suffer fools gladly, seeing ye yourselves are wise. For ye suffer, if a man bring you into bondage, if a man devour you, if a man take of you, if a man exalt himself, if a man smite you on the face. I speak as concerning reproach, as though we had been weak.
>
> Howbeit whereinsoever any is bold, (I speak foolishly,) I am bold also. Are they Hebrews? so am I. Are they Israelites? so am I. Are they the seed of Abraham? so am I. Are they ministers of Christ? (I speak as a fool) I am more; in labours more abundant, in stripes above measure, in prisons more frequent, in deaths oft. Of the Jews five times received I forty stripes save one. Thrice was I beaten with rods, once was I stoned, thrice I suffered shipwreck, a night and a day I have been in the deep; In journeyings often, in perils of waters, in perils of robbers, in perils by mine own countrymen, in perils by the heathen, in perils in the city, in perils in the wilderness, in perils in the sea, in perils among false brethren; In weariness and painfulness,

in watchings often, in hunger and thirst, in fastings often, in cold and nakedness.

Beside those things that are without, that which cometh upon me daily, the care of all the churches. Who is weak, and I am not weak? who is offended, and I burn not? If I must needs glory, I will glory of the things which concern mine infirmities. The God and Father of our Lord Jesus Christ, which is blessed for evermore, knoweth that I lie not. In Damascus the governor under Aretas the king kept the city of the Damascenes with a garrison, desirous to apprehend me: And through a window in a basket was I let down by the wall, and escaped his hands. (2 Cor. 11:16–33)

No one should take Paul for a fool, but Paul begins by begging to act like one for a minute (v. 16). He is not following an explicit example of Christ, but rather has decided to boast in an artificial manner, carefully labeling it as such (v. 17). He is imitating Christ truly while imitating the false teachers ironically. Since everybody around here is plumping their resume, Paul has decided to do the same (v. 18)—and since the Corinthians tolerate fools so readily, perhaps this kind of behavior will get them to tolerate Paul (v. 19). If a teacher abuses them, the Corinthians eat it up. Maybe Paul should slap them in the face to win their affections (v. 20). Paul is embarrassed that he is too weak an apostle to treat them like that (v. 21). But where these false ones are bold enough to brag, Paul can keep pace with them (v. 21). In all their checklist shine, Paul is their equal (v. 22).

But then Paul gets onto his alternative resume, listing the things the false apostles would never even think to put on theirs (v. 23a). Paul had gotten beaten, jailed, and threatened many more times than they had (v. 23b). He was flogged by the Jews, 195 strokes (v. 24). He was beaten with rods three times, stoned once, shipwrecked three times, and once left adrift at sea (v. 25). He was always on the road, and he was endangered by water, robbers, Jews, and Gentiles, whether he was in the city, in the country, at sea, or among false brothers (v. 26). What's more, there were the afflictions that resulted from his own vigilance: his watch-care, fasting, and going without normal comforts (v. 27). And on top of everything else, Paul had the constant pastoral anxiety of how his children in Christ were doing (vv. 28–29)—because being a pastor means watching people make bad choices for a living.

So if Paul is forced into a boasting glory, he is going to do it with regard to all his scars and frailties (v. 30). Paul then takes a solemn oath as he signs the bottom of his resume (v. 31)—God is witness.

And then he says, P.S. I almost forgot that time the *ethnarch* at Damascus had a garrison out hunting for me (v. 32). But Paul successfully evaded arrest as he was lowered from the city wall in a basket (v. 33). He got away safely, but it was a crowning indignity. For the sake of convenience, we will call this his Romans 13 basket, the one he used to evade arrest from the established authority.

When Paul says that he can stay with the false apostles on their own ground, step-for-step, he is referring to things that it makes no sense to boast about.

> For who makes you differ from another? And what do
> you have that you did not receive? Now if you did in-
> deed receive it, why do you boast as if you had not re-
> ceived it? (1 Cor. 4:7, NKJV)

Paul was a Hebrew too. He was an Israelite also. He was a son of Abraham. This was like being proud of having two kidneys and ten toes.

But when it comes to Paul's endurance for the gospel, boasting makes some kind of sense on the surface. Endur-ance requires continual effort. But even here, Paul says, there is no room for boasting: "For if I preach the gospel, I have nothing to boast of, for necessity is laid upon me; yes, woe is me if I do not preach the gospel!" (1 Cor. 9:16, NKJV). Paul is in the same bind as Jeremiah. Whenever Jer-emiah spoke in the name of the Lord, abuse was heaped on him—and so he would resolve to shut up. But when he did *that*, God's Word was a burning fire in his bones (Jer. 20:9). It wasn't *possible* to shut up.

And this is why Paul regularly asks his people to pray for his deliverance and boldness in preaching the gospel (Rom. 15:30–32; 2 Cor. 1:10–11; Eph. 6:18–20; Phil. 1:19; Col. 4:2–4; 1 Thess. 5:25; 2 Thess. 3:1–2). Paul was not over-coming stage fright or wrestling with his butterflies. He was wrestling with principalities and powers—earthly kings and the powers behind them.

A couple times in this litany of affliction, Paul mentions dangers "from the side," as it were: shipwrecks and rob-bers. But the overwhelming number of strokes applied to *the back of the man who wrote Romans 13* were applied to him by the established and respected *authorities*, and they were applied because of his sturdy defiance of them. Paul was not, shall we say, on their good side. The authorities found him *angular*. Paul was lowered in a basket from the city walls while the governor had search parties out looking for him and checkpoints at the gates to keep him from leaving. That's called evading arrest. That's called running a roadblock. That's called not turning yourself in at the police station. And it's also fully consistent with Romans 13.

We are Christians, and this means that we confess that Christ is Lord. This confession entails the corollary that Caesar is not Lord. Caesar is to be respected and honored *as Caesar*, but never as Lord. Sooner die than confess him as Lord. Christ is the one who rose from the dead, and all eyes must turn to Him.

2 CORINTHIANS 12:1-21

WATER TO WINE, WEAKNESS TO STRENGTH

The previous section of this letter ended with Paul being lowered from a city wall in a basket, a humiliating departure from the city of Damascus. In this next section, Paul describes being carried up into the highest heaven, providing us with a stark contrast indeed. This particular boast was necessary because apparently the false apostles were trumpeting some of *their* ecstatic experiences, and Paul needed to spike the guns of their argument.

> It is not expedient for me doubtless to glory. I will come
> to visions and revelations of the Lord. I knew a man in
> Christ above fourteen years ago, (whether in the body,
> I cannot tell; or whether out of the body, I cannot tell:

God knoweth;) such an one caught up to the third heaven. And I knew such a man, (whether in the body, or out of the body, I cannot tell: God knoweth;) How that he was caught up into paradise, and heard unspeakable words, which it is not lawful for a man to utter. Of such an one will I glory: yet of myself I will not glory, but in mine infirmities. For though I would desire to glory, I shall not be a fool; for I will say the truth: but now I forbear, lest any man should think of me above that which he seeth me to be, or that he heareth of me. And lest I should be exalted above measure through the abundance of the revelations, there was given to me a thorn in the flesh, the messenger of Satan to buffet me, lest I should be exalted above measure. For this thing I besought the Lord thrice, that it might depart from me. And he said unto me, My grace is sufficient for thee: for my strength is made perfect in weakness. Most gladly therefore will I rather glory in my infirmities, that the power of Christ may rest upon me. Therefore I take pleasure in infirmities, in reproaches, in necessities, in persecutions, in distresses for Christ's sake: for when I am weak, then am I strong. (2 Cor. 12:1–10)

All this boasting is no good, Paul says, so here comes a little more of it (v. 1). Let us talk about visions and revelations. This is embarrassing, so Paul shifts to the third person (although he comes back to the first person in verse 7). He makes a point to say that he is not doing this because it somehow establishes *his* credibility, but rather because it trumps the way the false teachers want to establish *their* credibility. Paul knows a man who fourteen years or so before was caught up into the third heaven (v. 2). (Fourteen years prior would have been around A.D. 42, prior to the first missionary journey.) He is not sure if it was in the body or not—only God knows (v. 3). This man in paradise heard things there that would not be lawful for him to repeat down here (v. 4).

Paul is willing to boast of a "third-person me," but if it comes to "first-person me," the only thing he can brag about are his infirmities (v. 5). Even if Paul wanted to boast, which he doesn't, he will not go too far into that folly. He is going to lay off, in case anyone thinks more highly of Paul than what they can see or hear for themselves (v. 6). The vision of paradise was *so* exalted that God gave him a thorn in the flesh to keep him centered and steady (v. 7). Paul sought the Lord three times about that thorn's removal (v. 8)—as the Lord Himself had done in Gethsemane regarding the cup that He had to drink. God, in His severe mercy, said *no*.

The reason was that God's grace is perfected in weakness (v. 9a). Our infirmities are the kiln in which God solidifies the final gloss. In submission to this decision, Paul says that he will gladly glory in his infirmities, so that the power of Christ might rest upon him (v. 9b). He then says it another way. He takes pleasure in infirmities, reproaches, necessities, persecutions, and distresses; these are all leaves in his laurel crown. All this is for Christ's sake, because when I am weak, Paul says, in that moment I am strong (v. 10).

The reference to paradise here is one of three references in the New Testament. In Revelation 2:7, it is the location of the Tree of Life. In Luke 23:43, Christ tells the thief on the cross that they will be together that day in paradise. And in this place, Paul equates paradise with the third heaven (vv. 2, 4).

But Jesus also said that He was going to spend three days and three nights in the heart of the earth (Matt. 12:40), which would make paradise subterranean, like Abraham's bosom (Luke 16:22). So I take the Lord's resurrection and ascension as the time when He transferred paradise up to the heavenly realms (Matt. 27:52; Eph. 4:8–10).

The Scripture uses the term "heavens" to refer to different realities. "Heavens" can refer to what we call the sky. Moses calls birds creatures of *heaven* (Gen. 6:7). Jesus says the same thing (Matt. 6:26). And James says that heaven is where rain comes from (James 5:18). A second use of heaven refers to what is commonly called outer space. After describing the sun going dark, and the moon not giving its light, Jesus says that the powers of the heavens will be shaken (Matt. 24:29). In the book of Deuteronomy, the Israelites are told to resist the temptation to worship these celestial bodies (Deut. 4:19). Throughout Scripture, the stars are called the host of *heaven* (e.g., Deut. 17:3; 2 Kings 23:5).

But there is more. A third heaven contains realities beyond what we can see—called the highest heaven (Deut. 10:14), or the heaven of heavens (Ps. 148:4). This third heaven is where God's presence is manifested. He cannot be contained by the heaven of heavens (1 Kings 8:27), and yet God's presence is somehow localized there: "For Christ is not entered into the holy places made with hands, which are the figures of the true; *but into heaven itself,* now to appear in *the presence of God* for us" (Heb. 9:24; cf. Heb 8:1; Acts 7:55). Also keep in mind that Heaven is a place that can be simply "opened" to us—as it was at Christ's baptism (Luke 3:21), or Stephen's martyrdom (Acts 7:56), or Peter's vision (Acts 10:11).

Considering all these things, we should identify the "third heaven" that Paul mentions here (2 Cor. 12:2, 4) as the highest Heaven, where the presence of God is manifested.

> Seeing then that we have a great high priest, *that is passed into the heavens*, Jesus the Son of God, let us hold fast our profession. (Heb. 4:14)

There has been much speculation about Paul's mystery thorn. What was it? Calvin once said that the apostle Paul had "troubles hard enough to break a thousand hearts." But this exalted experience had happened before a lot of those troubles had occurred, and it was *such* an ecstatic event that God gave Paul a thorn in the flesh to keep him from getting exalted "above measure." (We should always keep one eye on the false apostles. If Paul needed a great trial to keep him from getting conceited, what could be done for those false brothers who were *already* conceited to start with?)

We cannot say for certain what that thorn was. My supposition is that it was failing eyesight or some sort of eye disease. This would have been a great grief to a scholar like Paul—to whom certain manuscripts were precious, for example (2 Tim. 4:13). Paul says that the Galatians had loved him so much they would have donated their *eyes* to him (Gal. 4:15). He signed that same letter in large letters

(Gal. 6:11), which may have been because of eyesight. And when he was on trial in the Sanhedrin, he could not see or identify who the high priest was (Acts 23:5).

In the economy of God, water is turned to wine, and weakness to strength. As we've seen, power in weakness is one of Paul's great themes in his instruction of the Corinthian church. We have our treasure in jars of clay.

And so what is Paul's response to God's refusal to remove his thorn? He says some remarkable things. He says that he boasts in his infirmities, and that he does so gladly (v. 9). And he does this *so that* the power of Christ might rest upon him. This is not just an admirable stoicism. Paul is pursuing glory. Whatever else this infirmity might do, it bears the weight of the power of Christ. And this is why Paul *takes pleasure in* his troubles—*not* out of masochism, but rather as someone who knows how to read the story he is in. The power of Christ rests upon the weakness of men.

APOSTOLIC INSIGNIA

As we approach the end of this epistle, Paul gives us a good summary of what constitutes the apostolic insignia. There are three elements that can be seen here in our text: apostolic *signs* (works of power and authority), apostolic *sacrifice* (Paul's willingness to spend himself dry for the Corinthians), and apostolic *fears* (his ongoing concern for their spiritual well-being).

> I am become a fool in glorying; ye have compelled me: for I ought to have been commended of you: for in

nothing am I behind the very chiefest apostles, though I be nothing. Truly the signs of an apostle were wrought among you in all patience, in signs, and wonders, and mighty deeds. For what is it wherein ye were inferior to other churches, except it be that I myself was not burdensome to you? forgive me this wrong.

Behold, the third time I am ready to come to you; and I will not be burdensome to you: for I seek not yours, but you: for the children ought not to lay up for the parents, but the parents for the children. And I will very gladly spend and be spent for you; though the more abundantly I love you, the less I be loved. But be it so, I did not burden you: nevertheless, being crafty, I caught you with guile. Did I make a gain of you by any of them whom I sent unto you? I desired Titus, and with him I sent a brother. Did Titus make a gain of you? walked we not in the same spirit? walked we not in the same steps?

Again, think ye that we excuse ourselves unto you? we speak before God in Christ: but we do all things, dearly beloved, for your edifying. For I fear, lest, when I come, I shall not find you such as I would, and that I shall be found unto you such as ye would not: lest there be debates, envyings, wraths, strifes, backbitings, whisperings, swellings, tumults: And lest, when I come again, my God will humble me among you, and that I shall bewail many which have sinned already, and have not repented of the uncleanness and fornication and lasciviousness which they have committed. (2 Cor. 12:11–21)

It was acting the part of a fool for Paul to commend himself to the Corinthians the way he was doing, because by rights they should have been his letter of commendation (v. 11a; cf. 2 Cor. 3:2). And although Paul is a zero, at least he was ahead of his adversaries (v. 11b)—which makes them less than nothing. Paul then reminds the Corinthians of the miracles he did in their midst, true marks of a true apostle, and he mentions the fact that he did them in true perseverance (v. 12). Again Paul asks the Corinthians, how had he wronged them? Was it the fact that he had not taken any support from them? "If so, please let me *apologize*" (v. 13).

Paul then reminds the Corinthians once more of his sacrifices for them. He is their father, and parents lay up for their kids (v. 14). He would gladly lay up and lay out for them (v. 15)—but the more he loves, the less he is loved in return. He then addresses what the false apostles could say in reply: "Sure, Paul took no money from you, but that is because he is so slick" (v. 16). Paul retorts—did I take anything from you through my messengers (v. 17)? He sent Titus and the respected brother. Did they take anything? Not a bit of it (v. 18). Paul is not defending himself; he is defending the ministry of *the Corinthians'* edification (v. 19)—he swears it. And now we come to the third apostolic insignia: Paul's *fear* that his people have fallen backward into all manner of quarrelsome tumults (v. 20).

Two final things here. Notice that if Paul has to exercise church discipline, which he is willing to do, this would simultaneously be an act of authority and an additional humiliation to him (v. 21). But then notice what Paul tags as the underlying cause of all the quarrels of verse 20—it is found in sexual sin. He mentions uncleanness, fornication, and lasciviousness (v. 21).

This passage contains a passing comment that helps us sort through whether or not miraculous gifts are still extant in the church. (Please note the question is not whether God still has the power to work miracles—of course He does. The issue is whether He vests that power in certain individuals—it is the difference between healing and the gift of healing.) Paul says here that the power to work miracles is an authenticating mark of a true apostle. And if someone is a true apostle (in the Peter, James, John, and Paul sense), then they have the authority to speak for God, and that means they can write Scripture. But since the canon of Scripture is closed, we no longer need that authentication. So when it comes to the question of whether the power to work miracles is still in effect, the real issue is the place of Scripture in our theology.

Finally, Paul teaches us here about the mainspring of quarrels and tumults. He does this through a very curious comment as he expresses his fears about all the Corinthian disputes. Remember that these disputes could have been about *anything*—doctrine, finances, privilege and honor, and so on. Of course, what was driving Paul's adversaries was the simple fact that he was an apostle, and they were not. That was the foundational reason for the fight. But they would throw whatever was ready to hand. Paul mentions "debates, envyings, wraths, strifes, backbitings, whisperings, swellings, and tumults." That about covers the waterfront. But when Paul comes to address all their disputes, he flips over the flat rock in the garden and discovers the problem underneath is something else entirely. The source of all the Corinthian controversy was unrepented sexual sin.

Paul's love for the Corinthians was truly a Christlike love. The Samaritan woman wanted to talk about which mountain was the true mountain of God and related theological issues, and so the Lord brought up how many men she had been with (John 4:18–20). Whenever a sinner is feeling convicted of their sin, it is tempting to bring up something else to talk about. But remember what Paul told us about what Christ has done for us, back just a few chapters.

> For ye know the grace of our Lord Jesus Christ, that, though he was rich, yet for your sakes he became poor, that ye through his poverty might be rich. (2 Cor. 8:9)

Here Paul, following in the Lord's footsteps, says that he would gladly "spend and be spent" for them (v. 15). The life of Christ was a life of giving, not taking. "For even the Son of man came not to be ministered unto, but to minister, and to give his life a ransom for many" (Mark 10:45). The gospel message of this Christ must therefore walk in that same path. The ministry of grace is all about giving, not taking.

> Thanks be unto God for his unspeakable *gift*. (2 Cor. 9:15)

That word "gift" needs to be placed in celestial italics.

2 CORINTHIANS 13:1–14

TRUE EXAMINATION

There is a basic spiritual dilemma that confronts everyone who accepts the truth of the Christian message. If it is the case that there are only two final destinies for human beings—for the saved and the lost—and if it is also true that these two kinds of people are also found *within* the ranks of baptized Christian people, then the question is obviously this: "How can I be sure that I am among the saved?"

To that question, the Pauline exhortation in this passage is often applied: examine yourselves. Yes, indeed, do examine yourselves. *But by what standard?* Morbid introspection has often been indulged in with this passage appealed to as an authority—but that is not true examination.

147

This is the third time I am coming to you. In the mouth of two or three witnesses shall every word be established. I told you before, and foretell you, as if I were present, the second time; and being absent now I write to them which heretofore have sinned, and to all other, that, if I come again, I will not spare: Since ye seek a proof of Christ speaking in me, which to you-ward is not weak, but is mighty in you. For though he was crucified through weakness, yet he liveth by the power of God. For we also are weak in him, but we shall live with him by the power of God toward you.

Examine yourselves, whether ye be in the faith; prove your own selves. Know ye not your own selves, how that Jesus Christ is in you, except ye be reprobates? But I trust that ye shall know that we are not reprobates. Now I pray to God that ye do no evil; not that we should appear approved, but that ye should do that which is honest, though we be as reprobates. For we can do nothing against the truth, but for the truth. For we are glad, when we are weak, and ye are strong: and this also we wish, even your perfection. Therefore I write these things being absent, lest being present I should use sharpness, according to the power which the Lord hath given me to edification, and not to destruction. Finally, brethren, farewell. Be perfect, be of good comfort, be of one mind, live in peace; and the God of love and peace shall be with you. Greet one another with an holy kiss. All the saints salute you.

The grace of the Lord Jesus Christ, and the love of God, and the communion of the Holy Ghost, be with you all. Amen. (2 Cor. 13:1–14)

Paul founded this church. His second visit was the one where he ran into the surprise opposition of the false apostles. This will be his third visit (v. 1). When he comes, he will bring judgment, and he will apply the biblical standards of justice to the situation (v. 1). He warns the Corinthians solemnly that unless there is repentance, his discipline is going to be strict (v. 2). He will do this to prove the strength of Christ in him, as it is applied to them (v. 3). The strength of Christ is a death-and-resurrection kind of strength (v. 4), and Paul faithfully follows that pattern. Paul tells them to examine themselves before *he* comes and has to do it for them (v. 5). Christ is within those who pass the test but is not present within the reprobates (v. 5). And Paul is confident that the Corinthians will at least recognize that Paul's group is not reprobate (v. 6).

Paul wants them to pass the test, to do no evil, and he is not saying this for the sake of his reputation (v. 7). What matters above all is the truth (v. 8). Paul is glad to be weak, and he is glad for the Corinthians to be strong (v. 9). Paul's hope is that he might get the sharp things out of the way in the letter, and then when he is present with them, he might give himself to edification, not the demolition work of discipline (v. 10). He then gives a cluster of exhortations and charges in his farewell: be mature, be comforted, be likeminded, be at peace, and may the God of love and peace crown it all (v. 11). Greet one another with a holy kiss (v. 12). The saints send their greetings (v. 13). He then concludes with a glorious benediction (v. 14).

Before you set out to "examine yourself to see if you are in the faith," you must settle two other things first. First, what are you testing *for*? And second, what are you testing *with*? You are testing whether or not Christ is within you. That is the first thing; that is what you are testing for. Second, you should be testing yourself with the standards set by the Scriptures, and not by standards invented by your Victorian great-grandmother, or by some hedge preacher in a Kentucky revival two centuries ago.

So what do you make of Jesus? What do you think of Him? You should not be looking for certain ecstatic emotions or sentimental turbulence. We are talking about Christ the Messiah. What do you make of Him? What do you say of Him?

The standards of Scripture are what we test *with*. What standards can we take from the Scriptures? We know Christ is in us because we have believed in the name of Jesus (1 John. 5:13; Rom. 10:9). We know that Christ is in us because the Spirit was given to us (1 John 4:13). And how do we know *that*? Well, He grows things (Gal. 5:22–23; Eph. 5:9), and He kills things (Rom. 8:13). He grows graces and virtues, and He kills vices and sins. We know Christ is in us if we love the brethren (1 John 3:14). We know Christ is in us and we are converted if we have humility of mind, like that of a little child (Matt. 18:3). We know Christ is in us if we are hungry for the Scriptures (1 Pet. 2:2–3). We know Christ is in us if the sacrifice of Christ on the cross makes good sense to us as the power of God (1 Cor. 1:18). We know Christ is in us because of our growth in obedience (1 John 2:3). We know Christ is in us because of what happens when we disobey (Heb. 12:6).

Paul concludes this epistle with a wonderful Trinitarian benediction. The order of the persons named is a little different than the usual order. He begins with the grace of the Lord Jesus Christ. Our starting point here is the one who first came to us as Immanuel, God with us. Christ is the one who brings us to the Father, and this Father is the one who loved us.

And so it is that the love of God ("God" in this case referring to the Father) is mentioned second. And then, after we have encountered Christ and have been brought to the Father, we find that through the Holy Spirit we are in *koinonia*-fellowship with Him, and with all of God's people everywhere. And *amen*.

Find more books on the Bible. Go to

JOINCANONPLUS.COM